1

First published in Great Britain in 2005 by Orana Publishing Limited

www.oranapublishing.com

A CIP catalogue record for this book is available from the British Library.

ISBN 0955075106

Food photography: Simon Griffiths
Food stylist: Gabriella Cadden
Style and concept development: Patrick Crea
Layout and design: Reluctant Hero
Preface: Sam Reid
Food editor and indexing: Maggie Pannell
Legal advice: Lubna Azhar

The publisher extends their sincere thanks to Peter Rowland and his staff at Peter Rowland Catering in Toorak, Melbourne, for their gracious and generous supply of facilities and support throughout the production of this book.

Printed and bound in the United Kingdom by Butler and Tanner, Frome, Somerset.

tasteaustralia

an inspired cuisine from country to coast

tasteaustralia
an inspired cuisine from country to coast

Richard Bradfield

ORANA
PUBLISHING

Contents

Robust and vibrant, earthy and exotic, fresh and colourful; Australian cuisine is food for the modern age. It reflects the unique array of cultures, peoples and events that have shaped contemporary Australian society, and is also a wonderful celebration of diversity.

By embracing the successive waves of immigration to the continent over the past two centuries, Australia has emerged from its colonial history with an energetic and multicultural character. Indeed, Australian gastronomy has flourished with an intuitive sense of fusion that has set the national cuisine on a new trajectory from simpler, colonial foods, toward something far more eclectic and collaborative. From homemade country fare to the thrilling tastes of the ocean and the dynamic interplay of the global village, modern Australian cuisine is built around fresh and colourful produce that bursts with flavour, and is characterised by a healthy disregard for rules and traditions.

In *Taste Australia*, Richard Bradfield captures Australia's cosmopolitan spirit by capitalising on its eclecticism and expressing the nuances of this fusion in his cooking; delectable Mediterranean, Oriental and Middle-Eastern flavours are contextualised, along with the use of indigenous ingredients. As a proud Australian food ambassador, Richard has compiled an array of varied dishes that will not only introduce a fresh culinary perspective on Australian sensibilities, but also awaken, challenge and educate the senses.

With a swag of recipes that have evolved in Richard's kitchens over the years, *Taste Australia* helps us think beyond the obvious and immediate connotations of barbecues laden with shrimps and toward a fresh interpretation of how Australians eat today. Enjoy.

Sam Reid

brekky & brunch

Warmed muesli with dried fruit and yoghurt

Caramelised fruit salad with sweet mint yoghurt

Tomato, olive and mushroom fry on outback flat damper

Mushroom, bacon and thyme omelette with peppery redcurrant sauce

Australian shearer's breakfast with Virgin Mary sauce

Baked tomatoes stuffed with chicken and ham

Atlantic salmon and sweet onion rice congee

Apple and nutmeg rösti with sweet cinnamon crust and compote

Pan-fried banana and apple cakes with whipped butter

Apple and pear puffs with spiced cinnamon cheese

Banana, peach and pineapple muffins with warm maple syrup

Date and walnut brunch loaf with spiced butter

Milk twists with brandied strawberry crush

Prune, apricot and walnut buns with ginger butter

Warmed muesli with dried fruit and yoghurt

Australians are a pretty health-conscious bunch and the notion of a nutritious breakfast first thing in the morning remains as popular as ever. And it's not just the "iron men" on cereal boxes who perpetuate this image either – one look around most city cafés will prove our nation's (rather healthy) obsession with foods such as Bircher muesli, porridge and fruit salads.

Serves 4

85g raisins
50g dried apricots, roughly chopped
50g dried apple or pear, roughly chopped
50g prunes, roughly chopped
50g stoned dates, roughly chopped
50g dried mango, peach or pawpaw, roughly chopped
100g rolled oats
100g toasted almonds, roughly chopped
50g bran
625ml milk
250ml natural or vanilla-flavoured yoghurt

Combine all the fruit, cereals and nuts, mix well and divide among 4 bowls.

Bring the milk up to the boil and pour evenly over each bowl of muesli. Before serving, add a large spoonful of yoghurt over each dish. Decorate, if liked, with some extra dried fruits.

There's no great firm and fast rule for muesli other than going for a bit of variety. Other dried fruits can easily be substituted, such as dried figs, pineapple, cherries, blueberries or cranberries, depending on availability and your own personal preference.

Pawpaw

Caramelised fruit salad
with sweet mint yoghurt

I relish the chance to pick herbs from my pots at home and introduce their freshness and flavour into food – there's something very elemental about it.

Serves 4

for the caramelised fruit salad
225g caster sugar
200ml apple juice
1 dessert apple, peeled, cored and diced
225g strawberries, chopped
1 dessert pear, peeled, cored and diced
125g seedless grapes, halved
4 fresh apricots, stoned and quartered (pick another
   stone fruit if apricots aren't in season)

for the sweet mint yoghurt
2 tablespoons runny honey
250ml natural yoghurt
2 tablespoons finely chopped fresh mint

Using a frying pan over a low heat, dissolve the sugar in the apple juice, then increase the heat and simmer to form a light caramel. Remove from the heat, add all the chopped fruit, then mix well and allow to cool. Meanwhile, stir the honey into the yoghurt, mixing well, then stir through the mint. Serve the fruit in deep bowls and spoon some of the sweet mint yoghurt over the top.

Mint is known to sharpen the senses and complements the fruit salad with a natural verve that will leave you glowing.

Tomato, olive and mushroom fry
on outback flat damper

Once a staple snack for the roaming "swagmen" of the outback, damper bread is uniquely Australian. Traditionally baked in the warm ashes of a camp fire until it sounded hollow when tapped, damper bread is hearty, easily made and keeps well - no wonder it was a hit with the pioneers. Times may have moved on, but damper bread still makes a superb base on which to heap your favourite breakfast fry-up.

Serves 4

for the damper bread
500g self-raising flour
1 teaspoon salt
400ml milk

for the fry
3 tablespoons olive oil
1 large onion, thinly sliced
250g mushrooms, thickly sliced
2 fat garlic cloves, crushed
2 tomatoes, diced into 1cm cubes
125g Greek Kalamata olives, halved
2 tablespoons chopped fresh herbs
salt and freshly ground black pepper

Preheat the oven to 200°C (gas mark 6). Start the damper by putting the flour in a large bowl, make a well in the centre and add the salt and milk. Stir the mix with a knife, gradually incorporating the flour, to make a fairly moist dough. Place the dough into a well-greased, cast-iron frying pan, about 20cm in diameter, and bake for 25 minutes.

While the damper is baking, get the olive oil hot in a large frying pan. Add the onion, mushrooms and garlic and fry gently until the onions are softened and the mushrooms are lightly browned. Add the tomatoes and olives, then fry for a further 4 minutes until the tomatoes start to break down. Toss in the mixed herbs and season to taste with salt and pepper.

To serve, break up the fresh damper into 4 pieces and serve in large bowls with a helping of the fry.

Mushroom, bacon and thyme omelette
with peppery redcurrant sauce

Experimenting with new combinations of flavours and ingredients has become a hallmark of modern Australian cuisine. In fact, many of the best recipes that I've served on menus over the years have come about in just this way. Omelettes are a breeze to prepare and really versatile when it comes to fillings and sauces. This peppery redcurrant sauce has a unique harmony with the thyme-infused omelette – try it once and you'll never forget it.

Serves 2

for the redcurrant sauce
85g fresh redcurrants
1 teaspoon cracked black pepper
4 tablespoons sugar
100ml vegetable stock
1 teaspoon cornflour
4 teaspoons cold water

for the omelette
50g butter
2 rashers lean bacon, chopped
85g of your favourite mushrooms, chopped
1 onion, thinly sliced
1 tablespoon fresh thyme leaves
6 eggs, lightly beaten
4 tablespoons double cream
salt and freshly ground black pepper

Combine the redcurrants, cracked pepper, sugar and vegetable stock in a small saucepan and bring to the boil. Cook for about 8 minutes or until the currants start to soften. Blend together the cornflour and water in a separate basin to make a smooth paste, then whisk into the hot sauce. Cover and set aside.

Melt half the butter in a saucepan and gently fry the bacon and mushrooms with the onion and thyme, letting the flavours release, then cover to keep warm and set aside. Whisk the eggs lightly in a large bowl with the cream and salt and pepper to season.

Melt the remaining butter in a large omelette pan over a low heat, pour in the egg mixture, then steadily increase the heat to medium. Stir the egg with a fork, drawing the edges into the centre as soon as they begin to set. Keep the omelette over a low heat for about 1 minute, or until the bottom sets, then place the pan under a hot grill to cook the top of the omelette.

Once cooked, use a large palette knife to slide the omelette onto a plate. Pile the bacon and mushroom mixture in the centre of the omelette, fold in half and drizzle with the sauce. Halve and serve at once.

These Chilean Myrtle berries, also known as "Chilean guava," make a brilliant
alternative to redcurrants.

Australian shearer's breakfast
with Virgin Mary sauce

Conjuring up images of the hard-working shearers who helped forge colonial Australia, this antipodean counterpart to the full English breakfast lends itself well to the modern Australian palate.

Serves 4

for the Virgin Mary sauce
500ml tomato juice
50g butter
50g flour
1 teaspoon Tabasco sauce
2 tablespoons Worcestershire sauce
salt and freshly ground black pepper

for the shearer's breakfast
8 thick pork sausages
8 bacon rashers
8 eggs
4 baked tomatoes stuffed with
chicken and ham (see next page)

Heat the tomato juice until it is almost boiling. In a separate small saucepan, melt the butter and add the flour, stirring constantly for about 1 minute, then blend in the tomato juice, Tabasco and Worcestershire sauces, stirring until smooth and thickened. Season to taste with salt and pepper, then cover with a lid and set aside.

Cook the sausages and bacon, either under the grill or in a frying pan, until the sausages are browned all over and the bacon is crispy. Fry the eggs sunny-side up. Serve immediately with a helping of the Virgin Mary sauce and the baked tomatoes.

The Virgin Mary sauce lifts the traditional elements off the page with a Tabasco tang that will spike your senses - and may even end up curing a hangover!

Baked tomatoes stuffed with chicken and ham

Scratching for an alternative to the standard grilled or fried tomato? This baked chicken and ham version is a great way to decorate your plate. Savoury in every way; peppery and tangy, crunchy on top and soft in the middle. I prefer to use Virginia ham here for its full flavour and tenderness.

Serves 4

4 large beef tomatoes
cayenne pepper
salt
75g butter
25g flour
200ml chicken stock (or milk)
100g cooked chicken, shredded
50g Virginian ham, shredded
25g fresh breadcrumbs

Preheat the oven to 180°C (gas mark 4). Cut a small slice from the top of each tomato. Scoop out the pulp using a teaspoon and set aside, then sprinkle the insides with a little cayenne pepper and salt. Sit the tomatoes in a baking dish.

Melt 25g of the butter in a saucepan, then stir in the flour, and cook over a low heat for 1 minute. Add the chicken stock (or milk) and stir continuously until the sauce is very thick. Add the chicken and ham, season to taste, then stir in 2 tablespoons of the tomato pulp.

Fill the tomatoes with the chicken and ham sauce, then sprinkle the breadcrumbs over the filling. Cut the remaining butter into tiny cubes and scatter on top of the tomatoes. Bake for 10 minutes until golden and crunchy on top. Serve immediately.

Atlantic salmon and sweet onion rice congee

The influence of Oriental cuisine on contemporary Australian cooking is quite pronounced and has origins that stretch as far back as the Gold Rush of the late nineteenth century. Also known as 'Chinese porridge', rice congee is a simple and highly adaptable recipe. Despite its signature tang, the salmon won't hijack the other flavours of this dish; rather, it harmonises with the sweetened spring onion congee to form a truly blissful breakfast bite.

Serves 4

300g Atlantic salmon	500ml chicken stock
1 large onion, thickly sliced	300g short-grain rice
15g butter	3 spring onions, finely sliced
25g brown sugar	salt and freshly ground black pepper
375ml fish stock	black sesame seeds to garnish

Cut the salmon into small, bite-sized pieces, then put in a hot saucepan with the sliced onion, butter and brown sugar. Cook gently for about 5 minutes until the sugar has caramelised, then set aside to cool. The salmon should appear cooked through and starting to flake and the onion should appear dark brown and starting to caramelise.

Put both the fish and chicken stocks in a medium-sized saucepan, bring to the boil and then add the rice. Cook for 5 minutes, stirring constantly. Add the salmon and onion to the rice, then cook for about 10 minutes until the stock is almost all absorbed and the rice is tender. Add a little extra stock if needed or to make the congee soupier, if you wish.

Add the spring onions, reserving a few for garnish, stir and remove from the heat. Season to taste with salt and pepper, then cover the pan with a lid and allow to rest for 5 minutes before serving. Garnish with a little chopped spring onion and black sesame seeds.

Apple and nutmeg rösti
with sweet cinnamon crust and compote

While traditional rösti are usually prepared with thinly sliced or grated potato, this apple and nutmeg version makes for an irresistible breakfast nibble, with the sweet cinnamon crust forming a lovely crunchy texture around the soft middle.

Makes 4

for the compote
2 Granny Smith apples, peeled,
  cored and diced
175g dried figs, diced
125g caster sugar
125ml water

for the rösti
5 Granny Smith apples, peeled,
  cored and grated
1 teaspoon ground nutmeg
4 tablespoons caster sugar
4 tablespoons plain flour
2 eggs
4 teaspoons butter

for the sweet cinnamon crust
75g plain flour
50g caster sugar
50g butter, melted
25g fresh breadcrumbs
½ teaspoon ground cinnamon
25g flaked almonds

Preheat the oven to 180°C (gas mark 4). Combine all the ingredients for the compote in a saucepan, bring to the boil, then reduce the heat and simmer until the apple is soft.

To make the rösti, mix the grated apple, nutmeg, sugar, flour and eggs together in a large bowl. Heat a frying pan, then melt 1 teaspoon of the butter in the pan and place a quarter of the rösti mixture in the centre of the pan, flattening it out to form a rough cake, about 10cm in diameter and 1cm thick. Cook until the mixture is starting to set. Turn and repeat with the second side, then take the rösti out and place on a baking tray. Repeat, using the remaining mixture to make 4 rösti.

For the crust, combine the flour, sugar, butter and breadcrumbs in a bowl, rub together between the fingertips to form a crumble, then add the cinnamon and almonds. Place a handful of this mixture on the top of each apple rösti. Place the tray in the oven and bake for 10 minutes or until the crust is lightly brown on the top. Serve hot with the compote.

Nutmeg and cinnamon are beautifully fragrant spices that I love using. They're
real "siren scents" that will literally draw your family into the kitchen.

Pan-fried banana and apple cakes
with whipped butter

Bananas are one of the best foods in the morning. Palatable and filling, they contain an enormous range of vitamins and minerals - a natural multivitamin! Combined with apple, these cakes make great tasting fuel for the day ahead.

Makes 4

2 eggs
2 ripe bananas, mashed
2 Granny Smith apples, peeled, cored and grated
½ teaspoon ground nutmeg
½ teaspoon ground cinnamon
300g plain flour
1 teaspoon bicarbonate of soda
100ml milk, or as needed
8 tablespoons unsalted butter
maple syrup to serve

Whisk the eggs until smooth. Add the mashed bananas, grated apples and spices, then sift in the flour and bicarbonate of soda. Combine well. Add enough milk to make a thick mixture (slightly thicker than a pancake batter).

Place a frying pan over a medium heat and melt 1 tablespoon of the butter. Add a quarter of the mixture, then spread it out to form an even, 1cm thick layer. Fry until the mixture starts to set and brown a little on the bottom, then turn and repeat on the other side. Repeat to make a further 3 cakes.

Whip the remaining 4 tablespoons of butter until light and fluffy. Serve the cakes with a helping of the whipped butter and drizzled with maple syrup.

Apple and pear puffs with spiced cinnamon cheese

For many backpackers travelling to Australia on a shoestring budget, fruit picking has long been a source of extra cash and a free berth. In fact, my old stomping ground of Shepparton in southeastern Australia is one of the main fruit picking regions for apples, pears, peaches and tomatoes – it even has the largest fruit cannery in the southern hemisphere! The variety of fruit that comes with Australia's unique climate has spawned an equally diverse range of uses, from exotic fruit salads to bizarre smoothie combos and home comforts like these.

Makes 4

for the apple and pear puffs
2 Granny Smith apples, peeled, cored and sliced
2 pears, peeled, cored and sliced thinly
2 tablespoons cold water
1 tablespoon caster sugar
½ teaspoon ground cinnamon
½ teaspoon ground nutmeg
4 circles of puff pastry, each about 12cm diameter
1 egg, beaten
granulated sugar, for sprinkling

for the spiced cinnamon cheese
100g cream cheese
pinch of ground cinnamon

Preheat the oven to 200°C (gas mark 6). Put the sliced apples and pears in a small saucepan with the water. Add the caster sugar and spices, then cover the pan with a lid and cook for 4 minutes over a medium heat, stirring occasionally until the fruit has softened but is still holding its shape.

Meanwhile spread the puff pastry circles out on a baking sheet. Arrange a large spoonful of the fruit in the centre of each pastry. Fold in the pastry edges to form a rim around the filling, then brush the edges of the pastry with the beaten egg. Sprinkle with a little granulated sugar, then bake for 10 minutes until the pastry is golden brown around the edges.

Meanwhile, beat the cream cheese with the pinch of cinnamon. Serve the apple and pear puffs with a spoonful of the spiced cinnamon cheese on top.

Better known to us all as "Granny Smith," Maria Ann Smith is credited with introducing us to the apple that now bears her name. Maria stumbled across the famous variety in 1868 while tending to her family's orchard in Eastwood, New South Wales.

Banana, peach and pineapple muffins
with warm maple syrup

The likes of pancakes, crêpes and muffins are more A.M. indulgences than breakfast staples, but they do make delicious brekky treats for those special occasions (like Sunday mornings!)

Makes 12

125g butter
150g caster sugar
2 eggs, beaten
1 large, ripe banana, mashed
1 large, ripe peach, skinned, stoned and diced
50g canned crushed pineapple, drained
150ml milk, warmed
250g self-raising flour
¼ teaspoon salt
2 teaspoons bicarbonate of soda
maple syrup to serve

Preheat the oven to 180°C (gas mark 4). Cream the butter and sugar until light and fluffy, then gradually add the egg, beating constantly. Mix in the mashed banana, peach, pineapple and milk.

Sift the flour, salt, and bicarbonate of soda into the mixture and stir well. Divide the mixture evenly among 12 muffin tins, lined with paper muffin cases. Bake for 20 minutes until the mixture is cooked and lightly browned on top.

Gently heat the maple syrup in a microwave-safe container or in a small saucepan. Serve the muffins straight from the oven with a serving dish of warm maple syrup on the side.

Date and walnut brunch loaf
with spiced butter

Serves 6 to 8

for the loaf
175g dried dates, chopped
1 teaspoon bicarbonate of soda
200ml boiling water
50g butter, softened
125g caster sugar
1 egg, beaten
175g plain flour
50g walnuts, chopped

for the spiced butter
150g butter, softened
1 teaspoon mixed spice

Preheat the oven to 180°C (gas mark 4). Grease and line a loaf tin measuring about 20 x 10 x 7cm with baking parchment. Combine the dates and bicarbonate of soda with the boiling water. Stir well and leave to soak, until the water is cool.

Cream the butter and sugar for the loaf until light and fluffy. Mix in the egg, date mixture (including the soaking water), the sifted flour and the walnuts. Once combined, pour the mixture into the loaf tin and bake for 40 minutes or until the loaf is well-risen, golden brown and firm to the touch.

Meanwhile, whip the butter with the mixed spice until light and fluffy.

Allow the loaf to cool in the tin for 5 minutes, then turn out onto a wire cooling rack. Slice and serve with a generous helping of the spiced butter.

Milk twists
with brandied strawberry crush

Baking up a batch of piping hot sweet buns is one of life's simple pleasures. It might sound bizarre, but I've always found something quite therapeutic about kneading dough, so if you enjoy getting your hands in on the action, then try whipping up a tray of these for your next breakfast banquet. Take advantage of seasonal ingredients as they become available and experiment with any fresh berries you fancy.

Makes 4

for the milk twists
300g strong white (bread) flour
½ teaspoon salt
3.5g (half standard sachet) easy-blend dried
  yeast
½ dessertspoon sugar
175ml milk
30g butter
1 egg, beaten, to glaze

for the brandied strawberry crush
60ml brandy
200g fresh strawberries
2 teaspoons vanilla extract
100g caster sugar

Sift the flour and salt into a large bowl, stir in the yeast and sugar, then make a well in the centre. Gently heat the milk and butter in a small saucepan until the butter has melted and the mixture is just tepid. Pour into the well in the dry ingredients and mix together to make a soft dough.

Turn the dough out onto a lightly floured work surface and knead for about 10 minutes until smooth and elastic. Grease the bowl with a little oil, then roll the dough into a ball, put back into the bowl and cover with a damp tea towel or lightly oiled cling film. Leave to rise in a warm place for about 1 hour or until doubled in size.

Once risen, place the dough on a work surface and pummel a few times to knock the air from it. Knead the dough again slightly and then cut into 4 even-sized pieces. Roll each piece into a 20cm sausage, fold at the centre and twist around itself. Place on a well-greased baking tray. Cover with oiled cling film and leave again in a warm place, for about 25 minutes, until doubled in size. Preheat the oven to 220°C (gas mark 7).

Glaze each twist with some of the beaten egg, then bake for 10 to 15 minutes or until they are lightly browned on the top and bottom.

Meanwhile, make the strawberry crush. Put the brandy, strawberries, vanilla extract and sugar in a saucepan and place over a low heat. Wait until the sugar has dissolved into the brandy and juices from the strawberries, then turn up to full heat and cook for 5 minutes. Crush the strawberries with the back of a wooden spoon, stir well and cook over a low heat for another 2 minutes, then allow to cool.

Remove the twists from the oven, place on a large plate and serve warm with a dish of the crush.

Prune, apricot and walnut buns with ginger butter

Makes 4

for the fruit mix
85g dried prunes, chopped
85g dried apricots, chopped
1 small apple peeled,
  cored and chopped
50g walnuts, chopped
2 tablespoons brandy

for the buns
300g strong white (bread) flour
½ teaspoon salt
3.5g (half standard sachet) easy-blend dried yeast
½ dessertspoon sugar
175ml milk
30g butter
1 egg, beaten, to glaze

for the ginger butter
300g butter
1 teaspoon ground ginger
2 teaspoons icing sugar

First combine the chopped dried fruits, apple and walnuts with the brandy. Leave to soak while you prepare the dough.

Prepare the dough in the same manner as for the 'milk twists', combining the brandy-soaked fruit and nuts with the flour and salt before adding the milk mixture. Leave the dough in a large bowl, covered with lightly oiled cling film, in a warm place to rise for about 1 hour, then divide the dough into 4 equal pieces and roll each piece into a smooth ball. Place on a well-greased baking tray, cover with oiled cling film and leave again in a warm place, for about 25 minutes until doubled in size. Preheat the oven to 220°C (gas mark 7).

Glaze each bun with some of the beaten egg, slash the tops with a sharp knife, then bake for 10 to 15 minutes or until they are lightly browned on the top and bottom.

While the buns are baking, make the ginger butter by creaming the butter in a small basin until light and fluffy. Add the ginger and icing sugar and mix well.

Allow the buns to cool on a wire cooling rack or serve straight from the oven with a helping of the ginger butter.

tasters & starters

Battered aubergines and courgettes with caraway onions

Sourcrust tarts with garlic shallots and balsamic mushrooms

Double-crumbed Camembert with Grand Marnier marmalade

Three-cheese ravioli with fresh tomato and basil

Crab paté with poppy seed and Parmesan wafers

Anchovy mousse with wholemeal Pinot Noir biscuits

Scampi on chorizo horseback

Thai tuna croquettes with coriander, chilli and lemongrass mayonnaise

Herb-crumbed sardines with onion chutney

Steamed mussels with tomato, basil and salami

Citrus scallops on wild rice pilaf

Cured trout, pink peppercorn and brandy crêpe cake

Duck skewers with peanut sauce

Drunken quail on braised red cabbage

Pork and pancetta escalopes with vermouth cream

Rosemary-crumbed lamb with tangerine marmalade sauce

Lamb kefta with tzatziki and raisin couscous

Flowerpot sun-dried tomato bread

Battered aubergines and courgettes
with caraway onions

This is a beautifully balanced starter, bringing together the light subtlety of the battered vegetables with the caraway onions. Perfect for warm weather, served up with your favourite white wine.

Serves 4

for the battered aubergines and courgettes
500ml milk
50ml white wine vinegar
250g self-raising flour
2 egg yolks
2 large aubergines
2 large courgettes
75g flour for dusting
300ml vegetable oil for frying

for the caraway onions
2 tablespoons vegetable oil
1 large onion, thinly sliced
1 tablespoon caraway seeds
1 tablespoon brown sugar
2 garlic cloves, crushed
chopped herbs to garnish

Combine the milk, vinegar, flour and egg yolks and blend until smooth, then set aside for 30 minutes. Cut the aubergines and courgettes into 1cm thick slices. Once the batter has rested, heat the oil in a large frying pan. Dip the aubergines and courgettes in the dusting flour, then into the batter and fry for 3 to 4 minutes until golden brown. Fry the vegetables in batches, drain on kitchen paper and keep warm.

While the aubergines and courgettes are cooking, prepare the caraway onions. Heat the oil in another frying pan, add the onions with the caraway seeds, brown sugar and garlic, then fry on a moderate heat for about 10 minutes until browned and caramelised.

Once cooking is completed, serve the battered aubergines and courgettes with the caraway onions on the side and garnish with some chopped herbs.

Sourcrust tarts
with garlic shallots and balsamic mushrooms

This shortcrust pastry will complement a variety of flavours, so mix and match it with your favourite savoury fillings.

Makes 6

for the pastry
120g plain flour
60g butter, softened
30g soured cream
½ beaten egg

for the filling
15 small shallots
30g butter
2 garlic cloves, crushed
15 small button mushrooms, quartered
2 tablespoons balsamic vinegar
salt and pepper to taste
100g feta cheese
small basil leaves to garnish

Preheat the oven to 180°C (gas mark 4). Combine the flour, butter, soured cream and egg in a food processor. Press the pulse button, for a few seconds at a time until the ingredients form a smooth paste, but don't over-process the mixture. Wrap the pastry tightly in cling film and refrigerate for 15 minutes.

Roll the pastry out on a floured work surface to about 4mm thickness. Cut out 6 rounds, each about 12cm diameter, to fit into a 6-cup muffin tin. Grease the cups well, then gently press a round of pastry into each one. Place a square of baking paper over each pastry-lined cup, then weigh down with baking beans or uncooked dried rice. Place in the oven and bake for 9 to10 minutes or until the pastry has dried out. Remove and allow to cool.

Meanwhile cut the shallots into quarters and place them in a saucepan with the butter and crushed garlic. Cook over a medium heat for about 10 minutes or until the shallots are starting to colour, then add the mushrooms and cook for 10 minutes. Add the balsamic vinegar and continue to cook until all the liquid has evaporated. Season with salt and pepper.

Remove the paper and beans or rice from the cooled pastry cases and fill with the mushrooms and shallots. Return the tarts to the oven and bake for about 6 minutes. Crumble some feta over each tart, garnish with basil leaves and serve immediately.

Double-crumbed Camembert
with Grand Marnier marmalade

So, you want a dish with a twist that will show off your culinary prowess, eclectic taste and please the most discerning palate at your soirée? Camembert is lusciously soft in texture and oh-so flavoursome, but not overpowering, The Grand Marnier marmalade is a wicked addition that will leave your guests pleasantly intrigued.

Serves 4

for the crumbed Camembert
500g Camembert cheese
2 eggs
250ml milk
150g plain flour
150g dried breadcrumbs
3 tablespoons chopped fresh chervil or parsley
vegetable oil for shallow-frying
sprigs of fresh chervil or flat-leaf parsley to garnish

for the Grand Marnier marmalade
60ml Grand Marnier
6 tablespoons dark orange marmalade
125ml water

Cut the Camembert into 4 pieces, preferably squares or wedges. Mix the eggs and milk to make an egg wash in a shallow dish. Put the flour and breadcrumbs with the chervil mixed in on separate plates, then dip the Camembert first in the flour, then the egg wash and finally roll in the chervil breadcrumbs, until well-coated. Dip the crumbed cheese into the egg wash again and re-roll in the breadcrumbs to form a thicker layer, then place the now double-crumbed Camembert onto a tray in the freezer for 20 minutes.

Combine the Grand Marnier and orange marmalade in a saucepan, then add the water and bring to the boil. Remove from the heat and allow to cool slightly.

Heat a large frying pan with enough oil to shallow fry the Camembert. Once the oil is very hot, add the Camembert and fry until golden for about 2 to 3 minutes, turning only once to avoid breaking up the cheese.

Serve the Camembert onto plates with a drizzling of the Grand Marnier sauce. Garnish with sprigs of chervil or parsley.

Three-cheese ravioli with fresh tomato and basil

Ravioli makes a sophisticated starter for special occasions. It does take a bit of practice to get the parcels just perfect, but if you love the art of food, you'll enjoy the process and your guests will appreciate the end result. Australian cuisine has drawn much inspiration from the Italians over the years, so consider this a tribute of sorts! Lovely, handcrafted ravioli, filled with a delectable mix of cheeses – wonderful.

Serves 4

for the pasta
150g strong plain (bread) flour
1 teaspoon salt
1 tablespoon olive oil
1 egg, beaten
semolina flour for dusting (optional)

for the sauce
60ml olive oil
1 onion, roughly diced
2 garlic cloves, crushed
8 tomatoes, roughly diced and deseeded
20 fresh basil leaves, shredded into thin ribbons
salt and pepper to taste

for the filling
75g Parmesan cheese, grated
75g Brie cheese, rind removed
75g blue cheese, crumbled
salt and pepper to taste

Start off the pasta by combining the flour, salt, olive oil and egg in a food processor. Blend until small pellets of dough are formed (if necessary add a few drops of water to make the dough more workable). Place onto a smooth work surface and knead for about 5 minutes, until the dough is smooth and velvety. Add a little extra flour if the dough becomes sticky. Wrap the dough tightly in a polythene bag or with cling film and set it aside to rest for 15 to 20 minutes. Do not place in the fridge.

Combine all the cheeses and mix in a food processor to form a smooth paste. Season to taste with salt and pepper. Place in a bowl and chill in the fridge for a few minutes.

Roll the pasta very thinly into a 2mm thick sheet. This is best performed using a pasta machine, but if using a rolling pin, roll out the dough, fold it in half and roll again – then repeat twice more, until the dough is very thin. For an authentic finish, use semolina flour to dust the surface.

Cut the pasta sheet into 2 even pieces, each measuring about 32 x 24cm. Cut the first piece into 12 squares, then place one teaspoon of the cheese filling onto each square. Using a wet finger, 'paint' around each ravioli filling to moisten the dough. Cut the second sheet into 12 squares, then place one square over each filled square to form the ravioli. Press the edges together to seal them properly. Dust the ravioli in semolina flour (or a little strong plain flour) and lay out on a tray while you put a large saucepan of water on to boil and make the sauce.

To make the sauce, heat the olive oil in a pan, add the onion and garlic and fry until the onion starts to brown. Add the tomatoes and basil and toss the mix until the tomatoes start to break down. Season to taste. Cover and keep warm on a low heat.

Add the pasta to the boiling water and cook for about 3 minutes until it starts to float, then remove from the water and drain thoroughly. To serve, divide the pasta between 4 bowls and coat with the tomato sauce.

Crab paté
with poppy seed and Parmesan wafers

Serves 4

for the crab paté
3 tablespoons softened butter
250ml double cream
2 eggs
600g crab meat
2 tablespoons chopped fresh chervil or parsley
salt and pepper to taste
lemon wedges to garnish

for the poppy seed and Parmesan wafers
75g Parmesan cheese, grated
20g poppy seeds

Preheat the oven to 150°C (gas mark 2). Blend together the butter, cream, eggs and crab meat in a food processor until smooth. Season with a little salt and pepper and add the chopped chervil or parsley. Divide evenly among 4 well-greased ramekins. Place the ramekins in a roasting tin and pour enough water into the tin to come halfway up the sides of the ramekins. Bake for 30 minutes, then set aside to cool for 20 minutes. Increase the oven temperature to 180°C (gas mark 4).

Meanwhile, cover a large baking tray with greaseproof paper and spread tablespoons of the grated Parmesan into 16 small piles, about 3cm across and 2.5cm high. Lightly sprinkle poppy seeds over each pile and bake for about 6 to 8 minutes or until golden brown and crispy. Allow the wafers to cool, then carefully lift off with a metal spatula onto a wire cooling tray.

Once the crab paté has cooled, carefully turn the ramekins over and tip out onto serving plates or a platter, using a small, thin knife to separate the paté from the ramekins, if necessary. Garnish with lemon wedges and serve immediately.

Anchovy mousse with wholemeal Pinot Noir biscuits

Reined in by the sophisticated flavours of the Pinot Noir biscuits, this mousse brings the distinctly sharp saltiness of the anchovies into a refreshingly light bite.

Serves 4

for the anchovy mousse
50g drained canned anchovy fillets
2 egg yolks
1 tablespoon dry sherry
60ml light olive oil
125ml double cream
salt and pepper to taste

for the Pinot Noir biscuits
400g wholemeal flour
2 tablespoons caster sugar
1½ teaspoons baking powder
1 teaspoon salt and 1 teaspoon pepper, mixed
4 tablespoons olive oil
100ml Pinot Noir (or other light red wine)
4 egg yolks
2 tablespoons kalonji seeds

Combine the anchovies with the egg yolks and sherry in a food processor. Blend until well combined, then add the oil, a teaspoon at a time, until all the oil is incorporated and the mixture has thickened. Add the cream, blend until just combined, then season with salt and pepper and pour into 4 ramekins. Chill for at least 4 hours in the fridge.

Preheat the oven to 160°C (gas mark 3). To make the biscuits, combine the flour, sugar, baking powder and salt and pepper in a large bowl and mix well. Add the oil, wine and 2 of the egg yolks, stir together, then knead the mix until a smooth, soft dough has formed.

Roll out the dough on a lightly floured work surface to a 5mm thickness, then cut out small rounds using a 3.5cm biscuit cutter. Carefully lift the biscuits onto lightly oiled baking trays. Brush the biscuits with the remaining egg yolk and sprinkle with the kalonji seeds. Bake for 15 minutes until golden. Transfer to a wire rack to cool.

Serve the mousse in the ramekins along with the Pinot Noir biscuits.

Kalonji seeds, also known as Black Seeds, come from the Love-in-a-Mist plant.
Often used to flavour breads, they have a pleasantly bitter tang.

Scampi on chorizo horseback

The heavy flavours of the chorizo sausage form a spicy counterpart to one of Australia's favourite seafood bites. Match this dish with a crisp lager and relish the unfolding flavours.

Serves 4

12 raw large scampi or king prawns
15cm chorizo or spicy sausage
100ml olive oil
50ml balsamic vinegar
lemon slices to garnish
decorative lettuce leaves to serve

Carefully remove the shell of the scampi without removing the head or the tail fan. Cook the sausage in one piece in a dry frying pan over a low heat, until it is lightly browned and cooked through. Remove the sausage and cut into 12 pieces. Using cocktail sticks, secure the scampi around the chorizo sausage pieces, then place them in a hot, oiled frying pan and cook until the cut surface of the sausage is crispy and the scampi side is cooked through. Turn and repeat for the other side.

Serve 3 scampi per person, arranged attractively on plates with the lettuce leaves, sprinkled with olive oil and balsamic vinegar. Garnish with lemon slices.

Thai tuna croquettes
with coriander, chilli and lemongrass mayonnaise

These croquettes are positively more-ish. The crusty exterior contrasts beautifully with the soft tuna flavours inside and is set off by the spiced-up mayo.

Makes 4

for the coriander, chilli and lemongrass mayonnaise
4 egg yolks
juice of 1 lime
250ml vegetable oil
½ bunch fresh coriander, finely chopped
½ stick lemongrass, finely chopped
3 bird eye chillies, deseeded and finely
  chopped

for the Thai tuna croquettes
450g drained canned tuna in spring water
800g raw potato peeled, boiled and mashed
2 eggs
50g fresh breadcrumbs
1 teaspoon coriander seeds, crushed
pared zest of 2 limes, finely chopped
2 teaspoons chopped fresh mint
500ml vegetable oil for frying
chilli powder to taste
lime wedges to serve

Whisk the egg yolks and lime juice together, then add the vegetable oil very slowly, whisking continuously until a mayonnaise forms. Stir in the coriander, lemongrass and chilli.

Combine all the ingredients for the croquettes in a bowl and mash together using your hands until well-mixed. Using wet hands, roll the tuna mixture into about 20 balls.

Heat the oil in a wok or deep frying pan, then fry the croquettes until crisp and golden brown on the outside. Serve on a platter with a bowl of the spiced mayo and lime wedges to squeeze over.

Herb-crumbed sardines with onion chutney

Once again, this dish harnesses the strong with the subtle to form a superb flavour combo. Presented with the onion chutney, the sardines make for a visually scrumptious starter.

Serves 4

for the onion chutney
2 tablespoons vegetable oil
3 onions, thinly sliced
60ml balsamic vinegar
60ml brandy

for the herb-crumbed sardines
½ bunch fresh sage, chopped
½ bunch fresh chervil or parsley, finely chopped
½ bunch fresh oregano, finely chopped
100g fresh breadcrumbs
3 eggs, lightly beaten
500ml milk
20 whole small, raw sardines
300g flour
250ml olive oil for frying
salt and pepper to taste

First make the chutney. Heat the oil in a large pan over a low heat, then add the onions and fry gently for about 3 minutes, stirring occasionally until the onions are browned. Add the vinegar and brandy, increase the heat and cook until most of the liquid has evaporated. Set aside.

Combine the chopped herbs with the breadcrumbs and combine the egg and milk to make an egg wash. Over a sink, remove the heads of the sardines and clean the fish under cold running water. Carefully peel each fillet from the side of the fish, leaving all the bones attached to the spine as the fillet is removed. Coat each of the sardine fillets in flour, dip them in the egg wash, then the herb crumbs.

Heat the olive oil in a large frying pan, then shallow-fry the sardines until they are golden brown all over. Serve with a helping of the onion chutney.

Apart from being a great tasting source of high-quality protein, sardines are a heart-healthy fish, providing beneficial omega-3 fatty acids.

Steamed mussels with tomato, basil and salami

From Sydney Harbour restaurants to coastal campfires, mussels hold a special place in the hearts (or stomachs perhaps!) of most Australians. Shucking, steaming and scooping – preparing and eating mussels demands involvement in a meal and ensures a sense of occasion every time they're served, no matter where. The basil and salami infuse the mussels with a delectable, energetic flavour.

Serves 4

24 fresh mussels
1 onion, roughly diced
2 garlic cloves, crushed
100g salami, cut into julienne strips
1 tablespoon olive oil
250ml white wine
2 large tomatoes, diced
15 large fresh basil leaves, cut into ribbons

Scrub the mussels under cold running water, removing the beard at the same time. Discard any mussels that are already open.

Fry the onion, garlic and salami in the olive oil in a large saucepan until the onion is translucent. Add the mussels and continue to stir-fry for 1 minute. Add the white wine, tomatoes and basil, cover with a lid and steam for 2 to 3 minutes, until the mussels are starting to open, discarding any that remain shut.

Season with salt and pepper and serve up into 4 deep bowls.

Citrus scallops on wild rice pilaf

Australia's mostly coastal-dwelling population is blessed with an abundant variety of seafood available all year round. This fragrant, tangy starter makes a particularly popular choice in the warmer weather, along with a crisp white wine.

Serves 4

for the scallops
3 lemons, pared zest and juice
3 limes, pared zest and juice
250ml vegetable oil
250ml white wine
20 large scallops, shelled with roe removed
8 x 10cm twigs of fresh rosemary for skewers
2 tablespoons vegetable oil for frying

for the wild rice pilaf
3 tablespoons butter
200g long-grain and wild rice blend
1 onion, finely diced
750ml chicken stock, boiling
1 teaspoon cracked black pepper
1 teaspoon salt
lemon wedges to garnish

Whisk together the lemon and lime juices with the oil and white wine to make a thick emulsion. Cut the citrus zests into fine strips and add them to the mixture. Wash the scallops in fresh running water, then drop them into the citrus marinade and leave in the fridge for 3 hours.

Preheat the oven to 170°C (gas mark 3). Melt the butter in a deep, flameproof casserole and fry the rice and onion for about 2 minutes. Add the boiling chicken stock and salt and pepper, stir well, then cover and cook in the oven for about 45 minutes or until the rice is tender and the stock is absorbed.

Remove the scallops from the marinade and thread them onto the rosemary twigs. Heat the 2 tablespoons of oil in a frying pan, add the skewers and cook over a high heat for 2 minutes on each side, until the scallops are sealed but still fairly rare in the centre. Serve the skewers over a scoop of the rice with lemon wedges to garnish.

Like most Australians, I delight in the simplicity of seafood every time I cook it – few additions are required to create a fantastic dish and a memorable occasion.

Cured trout, pink peppercorn and brandy crêpe cake

I've prepared this stalwart and versatile fish in many different ways over the years (including a few riverside catches!) The flavoursome mix of the brandy, pink peppercorns and cured trout combine superbly.

Serves 8 to 10

for the cured trout (prep 24hrs in advance)
700g trout fillet, skinned with bones removed
300g fine salt (for curing)
300g caster sugar
1 tablespoon grated lemon zest
100ml white wine

for the crêpes
2 eggs
pinch of salt
115g plain flour
200ml milk
75g butter, melted

for the cake filling
600g cream cheese, at room temperature
30g fresh pink peppercorns
50ml brandy
½ bunch fresh dill, chopped

To prepare the trout, start by laying out the skinned fillets in a large shallow dish. Combine the salt and sugar, then coat the fish well on both sides. Sprinkle with the lemon zest and wine, then cover tightly with cling film and refrigerate for 24 hours.

When ready, remove the trout fillets and carefully rinse them under cold running water, being careful to remove all the salt and sugar. Slice the trout into very thin small pieces.

To make the crêpes, blend all the ingredients in a food processor for 1 minute, scrape down the sides of the bowl and blend again briefly. Strain the mixture through a fine sieve then rest the mixture for at least 1 hour. Cook the crêpes in a hot, lightly oiled 18cm crêpe pan, using about 50ml of the mixture for each crêpe. Stack the crêpes on a plate, interleaved with greaseproof paper, then set aside.

For the filling, combine the cream cheese and peppercorns with the brandy and dill, then blend in a food processor until smooth. Add the trout and stir evenly into the mixture by hand.

Lay a crêpe on a plate, spread with a 5mm thick layer of the cream cheese mixture, then lay another crêpe on top. Continue this layering until all the crêpes and most of the cream cheese mixture is used. Spread the final amount of mixture over the top of the last crêpe to give it a smooth appearance. Chill for at least 1 hour, then serve cut into wedges.

Duck skewers with peanut sauce

Duck has such a unique taste; richer and more aromatic than chicken, and a meat that works well alongside the buttery flavours of the peanut sauce, a real feature of this dish. If the weather is good enough, why not prepare these on a barbecue hot plate?

Serves 4

for the duck skewers
1 teaspoon finely chopped garlic
1 teaspoon finely chopped fresh root ginger
1 teaspoon finely chopped fresh chilli
2 tablespoons vegetable oil
2 duck breasts, skinned and sliced lengthways
  into thin strips
1 teaspoon paprika
1 teaspoon cayenne pepper

for the peanut sauce
125g crunchy peanut butter
125ml coconut cream
125ml water
1 tablespoon finely chopped fresh chilli
1 tablespoon curry paste
¼ teaspoon finely diced lemongrass
½ teaspoon crushed garlic

for the salad
250g bean sprouts
½ cucumber, sliced
bunch fresh coriander, leaves chopped
50ml sesame oil

Combine the garlic, ginger and chilli with the vegetable oil and thread each duck strip onto a skewer. Dip each skewer into the oil mixture, then sprinkle with the mixed paprika and cayenne pepper. Set aside.

Combine the peanut butter and coconut cream in a saucepan, mix together to make a smooth paste, then add the water, chilli, curry paste, lemongrass and garlic. Bring to the boil, stirring constantly, then remove from the heat. Combine the salad ingredients and toss well.

Pan-fry the duck skewers until golden brown and cooked through. Serve the skewers alongside the salad with a serving dish of peanut sauce.

To prevent wooden skewers from burning, always soak them in water for at least an hour before using.

Drunken quail on braised red cabbage

No, it's not what you think! I spent some time specialising in cooking both local and foreign game meats in Australia, and the ever tasty quail remains a favourite of mine. The rustic cradle of the braised red cabbage complements the sage and port flavours through the quail.

Serves 4

for the drunken quail
4 quail
bunch of fresh sage
250ml port
2 garlic cloves, thickly sliced

for the braised red cabbage
175g streaky bacon, cut into fine strips
1 large onion, thinly sliced
50g butter
85ml white wine
½ large red cabbage, thinly shredded
salt and pepper to taste

Cut each quail in half, removing the bones from the inside of the breast, then separate the thigh from the main body (preferably, de-bone the leg too). Chop most of the sage leaves, reserving a few sprigs for garnish, then add the chopped leaves to the port with the sliced garlic. Soak the quail pieces in the port marinade for about 1 hour.

Preheat the oven to 180°C (gas mark 4). Before cooking the quail, fry the bacon and onion in a large pan until crispy, then add the butter, white wine and shredded cabbage. Cover with a lid and cook over a medium heat for about 12 minutes, until tender. Once cooked, season to taste with salt and pepper.

Drain the quail pieces and place on a baking tray, then bake for 8 minutes or until cooked through.
Serve the quail pieces on a bed of the braised cabbage, garnished with sprigs of sage.

Pork and pancetta escalopes with vermouth cream

Although not commonly associated with cooking, vermouth combines uniquely with the pork and salty pancetta in this bold starter. Serve with plenty of bread to soak up the mouth-watering, creamy sauce.

Serves 4

for the escalopes
500g pork fillet
4 slices pancetta, halved widthways
a little oil for frying

for the vermouth cream
1 tablespoon olive oil
1 large onion, finely diced
125ml vermouth
250ml extra-thick single cream
bunch fresh parsley, chopped

to serve
8 slices of ciabatta bread, lightly toasted

Cut the pork fillet into 8 pieces, then, using a meat mallet or rolling pin, very gently beat the pork into flat escalopes. Lay a piece of pancetta onto each escalope, then tap it again lightly with the mallet or rolling pin to secure it to the meat.

Heat the olive oil in a frying pan, add the onion and sauté over a moderately high heat until the onion is light brown and softened. Add the vermouth and cook on a high heat to reduce until the liquid is mostly evaporated (be careful of the flambé effect during this process), then add the cream and reduce by about half, before removing from the heat.

Place a clean frying pan on the hob and get it very hot. Add a little oil, then pan-fry the pork escalopes on both sides, until well sealed. Put the sauce back on the hob to heat through, stir in the parsley, then add the escalopes to the sauce. Cook gently for another 1 to 2 minutes, then serve up with slices of toasted ciabatta.

Rosemary-crumbed lamb with tangerine marmalade sauce

There is a unique harmony here between the sweet citrus tang of the marmalade and the rosemary-infused cutlets that will inspire your dare-to-be-different side.

Serves 4

for the marmalade sauce
125ml boiling water
6 tablespoons tangerine marmalade
2 dessert apples, peeled, cored and diced

for the rosemary-crumbed cutlets
½ bunch of fresh rosemary
115g fresh breadcrumbs
3 eggs, beaten
500ml milk
150g plain flour
12 lamb cutlets
100ml oil for shallow frying

First, prepare the marmalade sauce by combining the boiling water with the marmalade in a saucepan, then stirring in the diced apple. Bring to the boil, then boil rapidly for about 10 minutes until the water has evaporated and the apple has softened. Allow to cool, then blend in a food processor until smooth. Transfer to a small bowl and chill for about 2 hours.

To prepare the cutlets, chop the rosemary leaves very finely, then mix the leaves with the breadcrumbs. Make an egg wash by combining the eggs and milk. Dip each cutlet into the flour, then the egg wash and finally the breadcrumb mixture.

Heat the oil in a large frying pan and pan-fry the cutlets slowly on both sides until the crumbs are golden brown, ensuring that the lamb is at least medium-rare.

Serve the cutlets piled in the centre of a serving dish with a helping of the sauce and your favourite salad.

Lamb kefta with tzatziki and raisin couscous

Thanks to the large influx of immigrants into Australia after the Second World War, my home town of Melbourne enjoys one of the largest Greek populations in the world. No surprise then that such stellar condiments as Tzatziki have wound their way into popular Australian gastronomy.

Serves 4

for the tzatziki
1 cucumber
½ bunch of fresh mint, finely chopped
500g Greek yoghurt
4 fat garlic cloves, crushed
salt and pepper to taste
juice of 1 lemon

for the couscous
250ml chicken stock
40g butter
1 tablespoon olive oil
200g couscous
85g raisins
50g toasted flaked almonds

for the lamb kefta
600g minced lamb
1 bunch of fresh oregano, finely chopped
grated zest and juice of 2 lemons
2 eggs
25g fresh breadcrumbs
500g natural yoghurt
3 fat garlic cloves, crushed
salt and pepper
sprigs of fresh mint or coriander to garnish

To make the tzatziki, start by removing the seeds from the cucumber, then chop the flesh finely. Put the cucumber in a bowl, add the chopped mint, yoghurt and crushed garlic and mix together. Season to taste with salt and pepper and thin the consistency with the lemon juice. Cover and keep chilled until ready to serve.

Preheat the oven to 180°C (gas mark 4). For the lamb kefta, combine the mince, oregano and lemon zest with the eggs and breadcrumbs, then form into 12 small meatballs. Combine the yoghurt, lemon juice and garlic and mix well. Place the kefta in a small baking dish and bake for 20 minutes. Remove from the oven, coat with the yoghurt and lemon mixture, then cover with foil and return to the oven for a further 5 minutes.

To prepare the couscous, place the chicken stock, butter and olive oil in a saucepan and bring to the boil. Add the couscous and the raisins, then remove from the heat. Leave to stand for about 5 minutes, until the couscous has soaked up all the liquid, then fluff it up with a fork and stir through the almonds.

Serve 3 meatballs per serving on a pile of couscous and dress with a little tzatziki. Garnish with a little mint or coriander.

Flowerpot sun-dried tomato bread

Basic and earthy, nothing ushers in a delicious meal quite like a portion of freshly baked bread. The ceramic pots help achieve a lovely quality to the crust that really locks in the magic flavour of the sun-dried tomatoes.

Makes 4

450g strong white (bread) flour
½ tablespoon salt
7g easy-blend dried yeast (1 standard sachet)
½ tablespoon sugar
150g sun-dried tomatoes, roughly chopped
240ml water
50g butter

This dish requires 4 small, unglazed terracotta flowerpots with drainage holes. Ideally, season the pots beforehand by coating liberally inside and outside with oil then placing them in a hot oven for about 20 minutes. Repeat this process several times before using.

Sift the flour and salt into a large bowl, stir in the yeast, sugar and tomatoes, then make a well in the centre. Gently heat the water and butter in a small saucepan until the butter has melted and the mixture is just tepid. Pour into the well in the dry ingredients and mix together to make a soft dough.

Turn the dough out onto a lightly floured work surface and knead for about 10 minutes until smooth and elastic. Grease the bowl with a little oil, then roll the dough into a ball, put back into the bowl and cover with a damp tea towel or lightly oiled cling film. Leave to rise in a warm place for about 1 hour or until doubled in size.

Preheat the oven to 220°C (gas mark 7). Once the mixture has doubled in size, punch it lightly to release any built-up gases, then re-knead the dough for about 30 seconds or so. Separate the dough into 4 even pieces. Knead each piece into a small ball, then drop into the 4 well-oiled flowerpots. Cover again with oiled cling film and leave the pots in a warm place for about 30 minutes or until the dough again rises to double in size.

Place the pots on a thick baking tray and bake for 15 to 20 minutes or until the bread looks crusty and brown. Cool the pots for a few minutes, then remove the bread from the pots, easing them round the edges with a knife, if necessary. Set on a wire rack to cool.

comfort foods

Potato, cottage cheese and spinach tart

Lentil, chickpea and rice casserole

Barramundi fillets in prosciutto blankets on polenta cake with pesto cream

Devilled chicken breasts with herb arancini

Plum-glazed duck on a stone fruit salad

Spiced fruit and beef tagine with couscous pilaf

Peppered rib-eye steaks on crushed garlic potatoes

Braised steak on tomato and black-eyed bean salad

Corned silverside on new vegetables with mustard cream sauce

Roasted pork chops on creamy mash with spiced whisky apples

Plaited Chermoula lamb on white bean purée

Kangaroo fillet served on beetroot pappardelle with smoked tomato and spinach

Potato, cottage cheese and spinach tart

The distinctive taste and texture of the spinach combines perfectly with the potato and cottage cheese here to form a mouth-watering bite. There's something very hearty about homemade pies and tarts in the winter months and this vegetarian option makes a great change to the more usual fillings.

Serves 4 to 6

for the pastry
225g plain flour
1 teaspoon salt
225g wheat germ
125g cool margarine, cut into
  even-sized pieces
about 85ml cold water
beaten egg yolk for glazing

for the filling
500g potatoes, peeled and cubed
500g spinach leaves
75ml white wine
250g cottage cheese
½ teaspoon dried basil
¼ teaspoon dried mixed herbs
¼ teaspoon ground nutmeg
1 teaspoon salt
freshly ground black pepper

Combine the flour, salt and wheat germ in a bowl. Add the margarine and rub into the flour with your fingertips until it resembles large breadcrumbs. Mix in enough water to create a firm dough, then divide the dough into 2 pieces, one-third and two-thirds respectively. Wrap the pastry in cling film and chill for 20 minutes before rolling out.

Preheat the oven to 180°C (gas mark 4). Roll out the larger piece of pastry on a lightly-floured work surface to line a well-greased pie dish, about 23cm in diameter. Cover with baking paper and baking beans (or dried beans or rice) and bake 'blind' for 10 to 15 minutes until the pastry is light golden. Remove from the oven and allow to cool.

Cook the potatoes in boiling, salted water for about 10 minutes until soft, then drain and mash. Wash and chop the spinach, then place in a large saucepan with the wine, cover and cook for about 45 seconds. Drain the spinach well, discard the cooking liquor and mix the spinach with the mashed potato and cottage cheese. Stir in the herbs, nutmeg and salt and pepper to season. Allow to cool, then place the mixture into the cooked pie case and smooth level.

Roll out the second piece of pastry to form a lid for the pie and place it over the filling. Use the trimmings to make a decoration. Seal the edges of the pastry lid to the base with a little of the beaten egg yolk, brush the top with beaten egg, then place the pie back in the oven for about 20 minutes or until the pastry is golden. Serve hot or cold.

Lentil, chickpea and rice casserole

Cooking for nutrition is very important to me, particularly when it comes to the family. Making meals both nutritious and flavoursome can require a bit of thought and ingenuity, but it's great to learn some staple dishes that not only taste fabulous, but are bursting with wholesome goodness.

Serves 4

2 tablespoons olive oil
1 onion, sliced
2 garlic cloves, crushed
200g long-grain rice
100g dried green lentils, rinsed
750ml vegetable stock
2 x 300g cans chickpeas, drained and rinsed

salt and pepper to taste
2 tablespoons chopped fresh parsley
2 tablespoons chopped fresh dill
100g feta cheese, crumbled
125g Cheddar cheese, grated
extra feta cheese and chopped herbs to serve

Heat the olive oil in a large saucepan over a medium heat. Add the onion and garlic, then cook for 5 to 7 minutes or until softened. Stir in the rice and lentils and cook for a further 2 minutes. Add the vegetable stock, bring to boil, then reduce the heat, cover and cook gently for about 20 minutes or until the rice and lentils are tender and all the stock has been absorbed. Add a little extra stock or boiling water, if needed.

Preheat the oven to 180°C (gas mark 4). Add the chickpeas, season with salt and pepper, then stir in the parsley, dill, feta and two-thirds of the Cheddar cheese. Place in a 2.5 litre casserole or baking dish and sprinkle with the remaining Cheddar. Bake for 15 minutes or until the cheese has melted and the top is golden and bubbling. If liked, serve with extra feta crumbled over the top and more chopped herbs scattered over.

Barramundi fillets in prosciutto blankets
on polenta cake with pesto cream

I love the layered flavours of the prosciutto and pesto combo. As always pesto is a feature flavour whenever used, but the cream softens its impact on the palate, and tops off this wonderful combination. Barramundi is a popular fish in Australia and ideally suited to this dish, but sea bass or cod would work equally well. Red emperor, coral trout, blue eye or trevally all make great alternatives too.

Serves 4

4 large barramundi fillets
  (or sea bass or cod)
8 full-length slices of prosciutto
100ml olive oil

for the polenta cake
500ml milk
100g polenta
salt and pepper to taste

for the pesto cream
200g pine nuts
4 garlic cloves, crushed
bunch of fresh basil
40g Parmesan cheese, finely grated
400ml extra-thick single cream

Wrap each fish fillet in two slices of the prosciutto so that it slightly overlaps, then set aside.

Bring the milk close to the boil and add the polenta in a steady stream, stirring continuously. Stir well over a high heat until the polenta has soaked up the milk and is the consistency of mashed potato, taking care not to allow the polenta to stick or burn onto the pan. Season with salt and pepper, then pour the cooked polenta onto a lightly oiled tray and spread out and flatten to 2cm thickness. Leave to set for about 30 minutes in the fridge.

Make the pesto paste by blending together the pine nuts, garlic, half the basil and the Parmesan in a food processor. Gently heat the cream and pesto paste in a small pan on the hob. Bring close to the boil, then slowly simmer until the cream is reduced, but taking care not to let the cream boil as this will cause the sauce to separate. Cover and keep warm.

Dip the wrapped fish in the olive oil and cook in a hot frying pan for 2 minutes on each side or until the fish is cooked through. Remove the polenta from the fridge and cut into large triangles. Also fry these until browned and crispy.

Serve the fish over wedges of the crispy polenta and drizzle over the pesto cream. Garnish with the remaining fresh basil.

Devilled chicken breasts with herb arancini

This spiced chicken has a lovely bite that sits well with the aromatic flavours of the arancini. A little bit of work involved, but definitely worth the effort. Served alone or with a crisp salad or fresh bread, it makes a delicious, filling meal.

Serves 4

for the herb arancini
50g butter
500ml chicken stock
1 onion, finely chopped
1 garlic clove, chopped
200g risotto rice
125ml white wine
2 tablespoons chopped fresh basil
1 tablespoon chopped fresh rosemary
2 teaspoons chopped fresh oregano
40g Parmesan cheese, freshly grated
2 eggs
250ml vegetable oil for frying

for the devilled chicken breasts
4 chicken breasts, skinned
1 teaspoon cayenne pepper
1 teaspoon Hungarian paprika
¼ teaspoon chilli powder
½ teaspoon dried thyme
½ teaspoon ground cumin
1 tablespoon flour
2 tablespoons oil
radicchio lettuce leaves to garnish

for the crumbing mixture
2 eggs
125ml milk
100g plain flour
100g fine white breadcrumbs

Start the arancini by melting the butter in a large saucepan while bringing the chicken stock up to a simmer in another saucepan. Add the onion and garlic to the butter and stir-fry until it starts to colour. Add the rice and stir-fry for about 1 minute over a medium heat, then add the wine and stir until the wine has almost evaporated. Add the chicken stock, a ladle at a time, stirring constantly and ensuring that each addition is absorbed before adding the next. Add the herbs and cook until all the stock has been added and absorbed and the rice is al dente. If not, add a small amount of water and continue cooking until the rice is ready (it needs to be quite dry). Remove from the heat, stir through the Parmesan and eggs, then spread out on a flat tray and leave to cool in the fridge.

Meanwhile, preheat the oven to 180°C (gas mark 4). Combine all the spices with the flour and the 2 tablespoons of oil for the devilled chicken breasts. Roll the chicken breasts in this mixture, then bake for 20 minutes or until the chicken is cooked through.

Once the risotto mixture has cooled, form it into 8 flat patties. Whisk together the eggs and milk to make an egg wash, then roll each rice patty into the flour, then the egg wash and finally, the breadcrumbs. Heat the 250ml oil in a deep frying pan and fry the arancini until golden brown and warmed through.

Thickly slice the chicken breasts, then serve alongside the fried herb arancini with a few radicchio lettuce leaves to garnish.

Plum-glazed duck on a stone fruit salad

You'll love this dish for the way the duck interplays with the strong flavours of the stone fruit salad. The juicy red plums are a real feature in this dish, adding a sweet delicacy and giving it a glorious, rich colouring.

Serves 4

for the plum-glazed duck
4 x 200g duck breasts or leg portions, skin on
4 ripe dessert plums, stoned and diced
125g caster sugar
4 teaspoons lemon juice
50ml red wine
¼ teaspoon ground cinnamon
¼ teaspoon freshly grated nutmeg
¼ teaspoon ground cloves
2 tablespoons honey

for the stone fruit salad
10 ripe dessert plums, stoned
3 peaches, stoned
3 mangoes, peeled and stoned
250ml natural Greek yoghurt
½ bunch of fresh mint leaves, finely shredded

To prepare the glazed duck, start by scoring the duck skin with a criss-cross pattern, using a sharp knife. Place the duck in a deep roasting tin and set aside while preparing the plum glaze. Preheat the oven to 160°C (gas mark 3).

Put the diced plums in a saucepan with the sugar, lemon juice, red wine and spices. Cover and cook on the hob for 10 to 15 minutes or until the plums are soft enough to be puréed. Cool slightly, then blend the plum mixture in a food processor with the honey. Spread about half the glaze mixture over the duck breasts, then roast them in the oven for about 15 minutes.

Meanwhile, prepare the fruit salad. Cut the plums into quarters, and thinly slice the peaches and mangoes. Combine the yoghurt and mint, place the mango, plums and peaches on a serving plate and drizzle over a little of the yoghurt mixture.

Baste the duck with the remaining glaze mixture, then roast again for a further 10 minutes or until the duck is tender. Serve each duck breast on top of a large portion of the fruit salad.

Spiced fruit and beef tagine with couscous pilaf

One of the things I adore about casseroles and tagines is the way they infuse your kitchen and surrounds with their unique aromas, and how their flavours are literally locked into the food. This spiced fruit and beef version is a magnificent way to start a cosy night in.

Serves 4

for the spiced fruit and beef tagine
750g thick-cut lean rump steak
flour for dusting
2 tablespoons vegetable oil
1 large onion, diced
2 garlic cloves, crushed
2 teaspoons ground cumin
½ teaspoon paprika
½ teaspoon ground ginger
2 bay leaves
1 small cinnamon stick
2 carrots, sliced
85g dried dates, chopped
85g dried apricots, chopped
85g prunes, chopped
500ml beef stock

for the couscous
300g couscous
1 Spanish onion, finely diced
2 tablespoons olive oil
2 tablespoons butter
½ teaspoon ground cumin
½ teaspoon ground black pepper
1 teaspoon salt
250ml chicken stock, boiling
chopped fresh coriander to garnish

Cut the beef into 2cm cubes. Try to cut across the grain of the meat to prevent the beef becoming stringy. Roll the beef in the flour until well-coated, then shake off the excess. Heat the oil in a deep pan, then fry the meat until well sealed. Remove from the pan and rest on a side plate.

Add the onion and garlic to the pan and cook gently until the onion starts to soften. Stir in the ground spices, bay leaves and cinnamon stick, then cook for a further 2 minutes, stirring the whole time. Add the sealed beef and the carrots, along with the chopped dates, apricots and prunes. Pour in the beef stock and bring to the boil. Reduce the heat to a gentle simmer, cover with a lid and cook for 1 hour.

Place the couscous in a large bowl with the onion, olive oil, butter, spices and seasonings and mix well. Pour over the boiling stock, then cover with cling film and leave for 5 to 10 minutes, until all the stock has been absorbed. Fluff up with a fork and garnish with chopped fresh coriander.

To serve, place a large portion of the couscous on each plate, topped with a generous helping of the tagine.

Peppered rib-eye steaks on crushed garlic potatoes

Rib-eye is one of the most flavoursome steaks available and cooking meat on the bone always enhances the natural flavours. The potatoes need to be a firm-textured salad variety. In Australia, we'd use Kipfler potatoes, which are low in starch and have a unique texture that makes them a great break from the average spud! Charlotte, Nicola or Pink Fir Apple varieties will do just as well.

Serves 4

for the crushed garlic potatoes
16 small to medium salad potatoes
200g butter
4 garlic cloves, crushed
3 tablespoons finely chopped fresh
 rosemary

for the steaks
4 rib-eye steaks (Scotch fillet steak
 with the rib still attached)
4 tablespoons freshly cracked peppercorns
2 tablespoons groundnut oil
sprigs of fresh rosemary to garnish

Place the potatoes in a saucepan of cold water and bring to the boil. Cook the potatoes for about 15 minutes or until they are soft in the centre.

Place the cracked peppercorns on a plate and press both sides of the steaks well on to the pepper. Brush the steaks with the oil. Heat a large, heavy–based frying pan, then cook the steaks for about 4 minutes on each side. For well-done, finish them in the oven at 180°C (gas mark 4) for a further 10 minutes.

Drain the potatoes, loosely wrap them in a clean tea towel, then crush them gently between your hands. Melt the butter in the pan, add the garlic and rosemary and cook gently for 1 minute until their flavours are released. Drop the potatoes into the warm flavoured butter, toss them around for about 2 minutes, then place them on a large plate.

To serve, place a steak on a helping of crushed potatoes and garnish with sprigs of fresh rosemary.

Braised steak on tomato and black-eyed bean salad

Braising is often reserved for cooking tougher cuts of meat, but I also find it a perfectly convenient way to prepare a meal. Get the recipe to the point where you can put it in the oven, then go and relax - all you need to do is wait for the timer on the oven to ring.

Serves 4

for the braised steak
4 x 200g rump steaks
400ml red wine to marinate
1 large onion, thinly sliced
2 garlic cloves, crushed
2 bay leaves
1 teaspoon salt
1 teaspoon freshly cracked
  black peppercorns

for the tomato and black-eyed bean salad
400g dried black-eyed beans
16 large cherry tomatoes, quartered
2 celery sticks, thinly sliced
handful of rocket
4 tablespoons olive oil
4 tablespoons red wine vinegar
2 egg yolks

In preparation, soak the beans in cold water and the steak in the red wine overnight.

The following day, drain the red wine marinade from the steak and set the wine aside. Preheat the oven to 150°C (gas mark 2). Heat a large flameproof casserole on the hob, add the steak and seal quickly on both sides. Remove the steak, add the onion and garlic to the casserole and fry gently in the meat juices until soft. Replace the steak, pour over the reserved wine and add the bay leaves, salt and pepper. Cover and bake for 1½ hours.

While you wait for the steak to braise, drain the beans and place in a pan of fresh cold water. Bring to the boil, cook on a rapid boil for 10 minutes, then reduce the heat, partly cover and cook gently for about 1 hour until soft and tender. Drain, then refresh them in ice-cold water, to cool, then drain again.

Mix the cooked beans, tomatoes, celery and rocket in a large bowl. Combine the olive oil and red wine vinegar with the egg yolks, then whisk together to make a dressing. Sprinkle the salad with the dressing.

Serve the salad topped with the cooked braised steak and some of the steak cooking juices and onions.

The black-eyed bean salad is refreshing and light, and a healthy complement to the braised steak. Black-eyed beans are high in soluble fibre, which is a great combatant of cholesterol.

Corned silverside on new vegetables
with mustard cream sauce

In Australia, corned silverside beef has always remained popular, being so cheap to buy and easy to prepare, not to mention a practical standby meal in the years before refrigerators! If unavailable, salted silverside or brisket work just as well for this recipe and partner wonderfully with the creamy mustard sauce.

Serves 4

for the corned silverside
1kg corned silverside
125ml balsamic vinegar
1 orange, halved
175g brown sugar
1 tablespoon black peppercorns
1 large onion
10 whole cloves

for the mustard cream sauce
40g butter
50g flour
4 teaspoons mild English mustard
85ml extra-thick single cream
3 tablespoons chopped fresh parsley

for the new vegetables
8 new potatoes
8 baby carrots
4 baby courgettes
4 shallots

Place the silverside in a large pot of water and bring to the boil. Remove the meat from the liquid and discard the water (this helps remove some of the residual salt). Replace the meat in the pot and cover with fresh water. Bring to the boil, then reduce the heat to a simmer. Add the vinegar, orange halves, brown sugar and peppercorns. Press the cloves into the onion to form a studded onion and add this to the pot. This will need to cook for 2 hours.

While the silverside is cooking, clean the potatoes, carrots, courgettes and shallots.

Once the silverside has cooked, remove it from the liquid and strain the cooking liquid into a bowl. Reserve 500ml of the cooking liquid as you'll need it later for the sauce. Pour the remaining cooking liquid back into the pan, bring back to the boil and add the vegetables. Cook for about 10 minutes or until the vegetables are tender and cooked through.

Start the sauce by melting the butter in a small saucepan and adding in the flour. Stir and cook for about 2 minutes over a low heat. Gradually pour in the reserved cooking liquid, stirring constantly to make a smooth, thick sauce, avoiding lumps and burning. Stir the mustard, cream and chopped parsley through the sauce, then remove from the heat.

Finally, remove the vegetables from the cooking water and serve onto plates. Carve the silverside on a board and serve over the cooked veggies, then coat with a generous amount of the mustard cream sauce.

Roasted pork chops
on creamy mash with spiced whisky apples

Pork has its own distinctive flavour and texture that is complemented perfectly by this spiced apple sauce. You'll love the combination of apple, cinnamon and whisky. And of course, what better partner to this delectable dish than some good old potato mash!

Serves 4

for the pork chops
pork loin rack, weighing
 about 1.2kg, with 4 rib
 bones attached
2 tablespoons vegetable oil
2 tablespoons salt

for the mash
750g potatoes, peeled and
 cut into large chunks
50g butter
125ml double cream

for the spiced whisky apples
4 dessert apples
200ml whisky
100ml water
¼ teaspoon ground cinnamon
¼ teaspoon freshly grated nutmeg
1 garlic clove, crushed

Preheat the oven to 180°C (gas mark 4). Place the pork on a rack in a roasting tin. Rub the oil, then the salt into the rind so that crackling will generate during the roasting. Pour water into the tin under the rack, until about 1cm deep, then roast the pork for 1 hour or until the meat is cooked through.

Meanwhile place the potatoes in a large saucepan of salted water, bring to the boil, then cook for 10 to 15 minutes or until soft. In a separate pan, boil the butter and cream until reduced by half. Drain the potatoes, then beat them with the reduced buttery cream, using an electric hand beater. Cover to keep warm.

While the potatoes are cooking, peel and core the apples, then slice them thinly. Combine the apples, whisky, water and spices in a saucepan, cover and cook gently for 10 to 15 minutes or until the apples are juicy and tender. Remove the lid and cook for a little longer, if necessary, to evaporate any excess liquid.

Once the pork has finished roasting, remove from the oven and separate each of the cutlets using a sharp knife. Find the point in the rack where the ribs can be separated and then cut through the meat. Serve each of the roast pork pieces on a pile of the mashed potato along with some of the whisky apples.

Plaited Chermoula lamb on white bean purée

Another brilliantly titled dish, and an equally brilliant combination of flavours. The Chermoula lamb plaits are a powerful visual centrepiece to this meal, while the natural nooks and crannies that form amongst the plaits ensure that the marinade is well drawn into the lamb, giving it a lovely, rich flavour. Ask your butcher to prepare the lamb fillets for you.

Serves 4

12 large lamb fillets

for the Chermoula marinade
1 onion, finely chopped
4 tablespoons chopped fresh coriander
1 tablespoon ground cumin
6 tablespoons chopped parsley
4 teaspoons Hungarian paprika
2 tablespoons turmeric
3 garlic cloves, crushed
1 teaspoon cayenne pepper
125ml lemon juice
250ml olive oil
salt and freshly cracked black pepper

for the white bean purée
300g dried haricot beans
125ml lemon juice
2 garlic cloves, crushed
2 tablespoons chopped parsley

Soak the haricot beans overnight in cold water. Drain, then cover with fresh cold water in a saucepan, bring to the boil and boil for 10 minutes. Reduce the heat, then simmer for about 1½ hours, until soft and tender.

Meanwhile, using 3 of the lamb fillets, pin the tops of all 3 together with a cocktail stick. Plait together and use another stick to hold the plait together. Repeat with all the lamb fillets until you have prepared 4 plaits.

Make the Chermoula marinade by combining all the ingredients in a shallow dish. Place the lamb plaits in the marinade, baste with the mixture, then leave to marinate in the fridge for about 2 hours.

Drain the beans, then purée them in a processor with the lemon juice and garlic. Add the parsley, pulse briefly and season to taste with salt and pepper.

Meanwhile, remove the lamb from the marinade and cook in a frying pan for 3 to 4 minutes on both sides, until it is medium-rare. Serve the lamb plaits over a scoop of the white bean purée.

Kangaroo fillet served on beetroot pappardelle
with smoked tomato and spinach

Kangaroo is a very popular meat in Australia these days and is making a name for itself abroad too. Kangaroo meat is very low in fat, and has virtually no cholesterol, making it a healthy alternative to other red meats. The beetroot pappardelle, smoked tomato and spinach make for strong, distinctive flavours that underpin this exciting meal. The secret to cooking kangaroo meat is not to overdo it, as being lean and low in fat it's quick to toughen if cooked too long.

Serves 4

4 kangaroo fillets
3 to 4 tablespoons oil for frying
salt and freshly cracked black pepper
Parmesan shavings to serve

for the beetroot pappardelle

2 medium beetroot
1 egg
200g plain flour
100g semolina
½ teaspoon salt
2 tablespoons olive oil
semolina for dusting

for the smoked tomato and spinach

100g woodchips, soaked in
 water overnight (optional)
4 plum tomatoes, halved lengthways
400g spinach leaves
¼ teaspoon freshly grated nutmeg
1 garlic clove, crushed
4 tablespoons white wine

Preheat the oven to 180°C (gas mark 4). Wrap the beetroot in foil and bake for 40 minutes, then remove from the oven and peel off the foil. Allow the beetroot to cool, then peel off and discard the skin and grate the flesh, wearing gloves so that your skin doesn't get stained. Squeeze handfuls of the beetroot over the sink until all the free liquid is gone. Weigh out 150g of this grated beetroot for use in the pasta.

Combine the egg, flour, semolina, salt and 1 tablespoon of the olive oil with the 150g grated beetroot and mix well. Using a pair of plastic gloves, knead the dough until it is firm and dry enough to pass through a pasta machine. Roll several times, following the manufacturer's instructions, then cut either by machine or by hand to form pappardelle (about 2cm wide ribbons). It is important to note that the pasta will need plenty of semolina dusting as it passes through the pasta machine as the pasta dough will be moister than usual dough.

Remove the woodchips from the water if using, then lay them around a baking tray and place a wire rack over these. Cover the tray with foil and place in an oven at 200°C (gas mark 6) for 10 minutes. Once the woodchips are hot, remove the foil, and place the halved tomatoes onto the rack. Reduce the oven temperature to 160°C (gas mark 3) and put the tomatoes in the oven for 15 minutes.

Place a pot of water on the hob and bring to the boil. Drop the pasta into the water and boil for about 8 minutes or until the pasta is al dente. Drain the pasta and coat with the remaining 1 tablespoon of olive oil, then season with salt and pepper.

In a small frying pan, heat the oil and cook the kangaroo fillets for 4 to 5 minutes, turning constantly until medium-rare and seasoning with salt and pepper.

Combine the spinach, nutmeg and garlic in a saucepan with the white wine. Place a lid over the top and cook over a high heat for about 3 minutes. Remove from the heat, stir until the heated white wine has softened the spinach, then drain.

Serve the pasta onto plates, lay the spinach and smoked tomatoes on top, then slice each kangaroo fillet into 3 long pieces and arrange on top. Garnish with a little Parmesan, if you wish.

for lazy days and
summer nights

Roasted red pepper, aubergine and courgette with tuna and white bean salad

Trio of vegetable cakes with garden salad

Fettuccine tossed in fresh basil, garlic and parmesan oil

Crayfish salad with tomato, chervil and mange-tout

Battered honey-sesame prawns on rice pilaf

Half-cured tuna on watercress salad with ginger and sesame dressing

Pan-fried salmon on Tahitian salad

Seared chilli-soy snapper with braised bok choy

Smoked chicken on Waldorf salad with redcurrant sauce

Chilled chicken stuffed with fig and plum, on peach and cherry sauvignon blanc salad

Cold chicken Maryland with macadamia stuffing, tomato relish and marinated asparagus

Roasted red pepper, aubergine and courgette
with tuna and white bean salad

Although everyone will be familiar with the delicate taste of these roasted vegetables, occasionally we have to lash out and add something that is truly magnificent. Truffles are generally not on one's standard shopping list, but I feel truffle oil is a delectable investment that everyone should make. With its hallmark flavour, truffle oil enhances food in a very special way.

Serves 4

for the tuna and white bean salad
400g cannellini or haricot beans,
  drained and rinsed
200g can tuna in brine, drained and flaked
100g marinated artichoke hearts, chopped
100g sun-dried tomatoes, chopped
85g Kalamata olives, stoned and chopped
3 tablespoons chopped fresh parsley
3 tablespoons pesto sauce
3 tablespoons balsamic vinegar
1 tablespoon white truffle oil
60ml extra-virgin olive oil
salt and freshly cracked pepper

for the roasted vegetables
4 red peppers
125ml olive oil
2 aubergines
2 courgettes
2 tablespoons dried mixed herbs

Combine the beans, tuna, chopped artichoke hearts, sun-dried tomatoes, olives and parsley in a large bowl. In a separate bowl, combine the pesto and the balsamic vinegar, then whisk in the truffle and olive oils. Add ¾ of the dressing to the bean salad, stir well, and season to taste with salt and pepper.

Preheat the oven to 200°C (gas mark 6). Roll the peppers in olive oil, and sprinkle with salt. Place them on a baking tray, then roast them in the oven until the skins are starting to blister and blacken. Remove from the oven, put them in a bowl, cover and leave to cool.

Slice the courgettes and aubergine into thick strips, and season with some of the mixed herbs, salt and pepper. Place onto a hot griddle or a frying pan that has been well-greased with olive oil. Cook until starting to turn brown on the underside, then flip over and repeat with the other side. Remove from the pan and keep warm.

Rinse the peppers to remove all the salt and gently peel the skin from the flesh. Wash away the seeds, then slice the peppers into wide strips. Season with some of the mixed herbs.

To serve, arrange the salad on plates next to the strips of pepper, courgette and aubergine. Drizzle with the remaining pesto dressing and serve with crusty bread rolls. Top the salad with extra pesto sauce, if liked.

Trio of vegetable cakes with garden salad

Despite being a devoted meat lover, over the years I've discovered some great recipes through cooking for vegetarian friends and customers. These vegetable cakes really bristle with flavour and nutrition and are super-easy to prepare. There are no hard and fast rules in terms of ingredients, in fact I usually just toss in whatever fresh vegetables I have around at the time.

Serves 4

for the chilli and carrot cakes
600g grated carrots
60ml sweet chilli sauce
2 eggs
30g flour
vegetable oil for shallow-frying

for the potato and corn cakes
600g grated potatoes
200g sweetcorn
2 eggs
30g flour

for the celeriac and leek cakes
600g grated celeriac
2 leeks, thinly sliced
2 eggs
30g flour

for the garden salad
10 cherry tomatoes, halved
1 iceberg lettuce, cored and torn into pieces
½ cucumber, thinly sliced
125g Kalamata olives, halved
2 carrots, cut into fine julienne
1 red or green pepper, deseeded and finely sliced
1 Spanish onion, thinly sliced

Preheat the oven to 180°C (gas mark 4). Combine all the ingredients for the chilli and carrot cakes and mix them with the flour to bind them to a malleable paste. Divide the mixture up into 4 portions, shape each portion into a thick, flat patty, then fry in a little oil on both sides until well-sealed. Repeat this process with the potato and corn cakes and then the celeriac and leek cakes.

Once all the cakes are made, spread them out onto a greased baking tray and bake for about 10 to 12 minutes or until the cakes are cooked through.

Combine all the salad ingredients and toss with your favourite salad dressing (2 parts olive oil to 1 part balsamic vinegar is always lovely). Serve the salad as an accompaniment to the vegetable cakes.

Celeriac or "celery root" tastes like a milder version of celery itself. Celeriac is really versatile and can be added to salads or used in soups.

Fettuccine tossed in fresh basil, garlic and Parmesan oil

Homemade pasta is a joy to prepare, and has become a popular alternative to packaged pasta as we search for fresher options. Of course, you can buy it fresh or dried ready-made if you're in a hurry, but if you have the time, it's well worth preparing from scratch yourself. Making pasta is such an age-old and simple process, and I especially love this recipe because it celebrates that simplicity.

Serves 4 to 6

for the fettuccini
6 eggs
600g semolina
1 teaspoon salt

for the dressing
1 garlic clove, crushed
150ml extra virgin olive oil
bunch of fresh basil, roughly torn
200g Parmesan cheese, freshly grated
175g sun-dried tomatoes, chopped
2 fat red chillies, finely chopped
125g pine nuts, lightly toasted

for the cooking liquor
5 litres boiling water
1 tablespoon salt
4 tablespoons vegetable oil

First make the pasta. Combine the eggs, semolina and salt on a clean work surface or in a large mixing bowl and knead into a smooth dough. A dash of water may be added if the mixture is too dry. Continue to knead the dough for about 10 minutes until smooth and elastic, then wrap in cling film and leave to rest for 15 to 20 minutes at room temperature before rolling out.

Divide the dough into 3 to 4 balls for easier handling. Roll each piece of dough into a very thin sheet, then fold in half, fold in half again and fold in half for a third and final time. Re-roll the dough into an extremely thin layer, and then carefully cut it into 1cm wide ribbons. Use a pasta machine if you have one. Sprinkle with a little semolina and carefully place to the side.

While you bring the cooking liquid to the boil in a large pot, combine the ingredients for the dressing in a large serving bowl. Once the cooking liquid is boiling, drop the pasta into it and cook for 2 to 3 minutes until al dente, stirring occasionally to prevent the ribbons from sticking together.

Drain the pasta, then drop it into the bowl with the dressing. Carefully toss around until the pasta is well coated, and serve at once.

Crayfish salad with tomato, chervil and mangetout

Chilled cray has a compelling, thrilling taste quite like no other and it must certainly be one of the pleasures of the deep. Let this salad fling with Champagne or your favourite white wine on a warm summer's night.

Serves 4

for the crayfish salad
2 x 1.5kg crayfish
2 large tomatoes
1 bunch fresh chervil, chopped
250g mangetout or sugarsnap peas, trimmed
1 bunch fresh chives, snipped

for the dressing
1 teaspoon mustard seeds
25ml white wine vinegar
100ml hazelnut oil
salt and pepper to taste

In a large saucepan, boil about 5 litres of water, or enough to cover both the crayfish. Once boiling rapidly, place both crayfish in the pan and cook for about 10 minutes or until the whole crayfish is bright red.

Once cooked, remove the crayfish from the water and place them in a large sink of ice and water for about 10 minutes, until chilled. Cut the chilled crayfish in half lengthways, then place the halves on a large tray in the fridge.

Cut a cross in the base and top of the tomatoes, then plunge them into a pan of boiling water for 30 to 40 seconds or until the skins are starting to split. Immediately plunge the tomatoes into the sink of iced water. Leave there to cool for about 2 minutes, then carefully peel the skin from the tomatoes by hand. Cut the tomatoes into quarters and remove the seeds. Discard the seeds and cut the tomato flesh into small cubes. Add the chopped chervil.

Blanch the mangetout in boiling water for about 45 seconds, then remove and plunge into the iced water to refresh them. Slice thinly, then combine with the tomato and chervil.

Crush the mustard seeds using a mortar and pestle, then tip into a large bowl. Add the vinegar to the crushed mustard seeds, then slowly drizzle the hazelnut oil into the mixture, whisking the whole time until a smooth dressing is made. Season with a little salt and pepper.

Remove the heads from the crayfish and discard, being careful not to damage the shells in the process. Remove the meat from the tail, add to the salad dressing with the tomato, chervil and pea mixture and mix well together. Divide the salad among the 4 shells and sprinkle with snipped chives.

Battered honey-sesame prawns on rice pilaf

Battered prawns make a fabulous summertime nibble at any rate, but I particularly enjoy this recipe for its glorious honey and sesame flavour. Of course, it depends on where you are and availability at the time, however I favour the larger king prawn variety. Whatever your choice, go for the best and freshest available.

Serves 4

for the rice pilaf
400g easy-cook long-grain rice
1 large onion, finely chopped
2 star anise
8 cardamon pods
1 litre chicken stock, boiling

for the sauce
100g honey
75ml water
2 tablespoons sesame seeds, lightly toasted

for the prawns
12 large raw king prawns (tails left on)
2 egg whites
75g self-raising flour
pinch of salt
125ml ice-cold water
vegetable oil for deep-frying

Preheat the oven to 180°C (gas mark 4). Stir together the rice, onion, star anise and cardamon in a deep ovenproof dish and pour over the boiling stock. Cover, then put in the oven to cook for about 35 minutes or until the rice is tender and all the stock has been absorbed.

Meanwhile peel, clean and remove the heads from the prawns. Whisk the egg whites to soft peaks. Sift together the flour and salt, combine the whisked egg whites with the water, then whisk the egg whites through the flour to make a thick, lump-free batter.

For the sauce, combine the honey, water and toasted sesame seeds in a saucepan and bring to a simmer. Cook the sauce for 5 minutes over a low heat until thick, then remove from the heat and cover to keep warm.

Heat the oil in a deep-fryer. Dip each prawn into the batter, holding them by the tails, then fry in the hot oil until golden brown and cooked through. Drain on kitchen paper.

Serve the prawns on a bed of the rice pilaf and coat with the warm honey sauce.

Native to both China and Vietnam, star anise is a powerful and distinctive spice.

Half-cured tuna on watercress salad
with ginger and sesame dressing

This is a great example of combining popular flavours that make for a refreshing, tasty bite perfect for the summer months. The mild chilli tang works beautifully with the half-cured tuna and the ever subtle mirin used in the dressing.

Serves 4

for the half-cured tuna
4 x 150g tuna steaks
60ml sesame oil
2 teaspoons salt
1 teaspoon dried crushed chillies
4 teaspoons sweet paprika
1 teaspoon lemon pepper

for the dressing
20g fresh root ginger, finely grated
1 tablespoon mirin
2 tablespoons white wine vinegar
1 egg yolk
50ml sesame oil
75ml vegetable oil

for the salad
1 red pepper, deseeded and thinly sliced
1 carrot, cut into fine julienne
¼ bunch fresh coriander
250g watercress, stalks trimmed

Roll the tuna steaks in the sesame oil. Mix the salt and crushed chillies with the paprika and lemon pepper, then sprinkle this seasoning mixture over the tuna. Turn and season the other side. Lay the tuna on a plate in the fridge for about 1 hour.

Remove the tuna from the fridge and cook for 2 minutes on both sides in a hot frying pan until the surface is just sealed. Put back in the fridge and leave to go cold.

Combine the red pepper and carrot strips in a bowl. Add the coriander leaves, then tear the watercress into small pieces and also add them to the bowl.

Place the grated ginger in a food processor along with the mirin and vinegar, then add the egg yolk and blend quickly. Drizzle the sesame oil and vegetable oil down the feed tube, while blending on a slow speed until the mixture is emulsified.

To serve, place a handful of the salad on each plate and pour over a little of the dressing. Slice the tuna steaks into thin pieces and lay these out over the salad, then drizzle again with some more of the dressing.

Pan-fried salmon on Tahitian salad

Salmon is a regular fixture at my house. It is such a beautifully textured, coloured and flavoured fish, and one of the healthiest bites around. Served on the Tahitian salad pockets, this salmon dish makes a fantastic tasting, light munch. You can buy the banana leaves in specialist food stores or markets.

Serves 4

4 x 200g salmon steaks
3 tablespoons vegetable oil for frying
2 tablespoons black or white sesame seeds
2 limes, thinly sliced

for the Tahitian salad
1 fresh pineapple, skinned and core removed
3 bananas
50g desiccated coconut
4 small banana leaves
4 teaspoons vegetable oil

Cut the pineapple and bananas into bite-sized pieces and mix with the coconut. Using a pair of tongs, carefully hold a banana leaf over a gas flame. It will start to turn a darker green and become quite soft and pliable. Once soft enough to bend and fold, place a quarter of the mixed fruit on the banana leaf and gently fold 3 of the sides into the centre to create an open-ended parcel. Secure the parcels with cocktail sticks. Gently fry in a pan with 1 teaspoon of the oil, until the banana and pineapple are starting to soften. Repeat to make 4 parcels. Keep warm.

In a separate hot frying pan, heat the oil, then lightly fry the salmon for 2 minutes on both sides until just cooked.

To serve, place a salmon steak over each banana leaf parcel and garnish with sesame seeds and the sliced limes.

Seared chilli-soy snapper with braised bok choy

Snapper is a really popular fish all over Australia and makes a great match with the chilli and the bed of bok choy. There are a great many varieties of snappers and in Australia, one of the most popular is called the red emperor or red admiral fish, coming from the Seychelles.

Serves 4

for the seared chilli-soy snapper
2 bird eye chillies, finely chopped
125ml kecap manis
  (Indonesian sweet soy sauce)
½ bunch of fresh coriander,
  finely chopped
2 tablespoons grated fresh root ginger
2 garlic cloves, crushed
60ml sesame oil
4 whole baby snapper,
  cleaned and scaled
vegetable oil for deep-frying

for the braised bok choy
3 large heads bok choy, washed
2 small onions, thinly sliced
2 carrots, cut into fine julienne
100g bean sprouts
50g butter
60ml white wine

Blend together the chillies, soy sauce, coriander, ginger, garlic and sesame oil in a large bowl to make the marinade. Marinate the snapper for about 30 minutes.

Preheat the oven to 180°C (gas mark 4). Separate the leaves from the bok choy and lay them in a shallow baking dish. Scatter the onions, carrots and bean sprouts over the top, then add the butter in knobs and pour over the wine. Cover the dish and bake for about 15 minutes.

While the braised veggies are cooking, heat the oil in a deep frying pan – the temperature of the oil should be around 165°C. Lift the fish from the marinade, then fry them in the hot oil for about 10 minutes, turning half-way through cooking. Once cooked, the fish flesh should be ready to flake and the skin should be crispy. Drain well on kitchen paper.

Serve the fish over a bed of the braised bok choy, piling the julienne carrot, onions and bean sprouts on top.

Smoked chicken on Waldorf salad with redcurrant sauce

Founded at the famous Waldorf-Astoria hotel in New York, I've adapted this salad with countless other ingredients over the years. Smoking the chicken with the hickory wood chips is optional, but it really does add another dimension to this dish.

Serves 4

for the Waldorf salad
2 egg yolks
2 tablespoons cider vinegar
250ml walnut oil
salt and pepper to taste
2 dessert apples, cored
2 celery sticks, thinly sliced
150g walnuts, roughly chopped

for the smoked chicken
4 chicken breasts, skin on
bunch of fresh thyme
100g salt
125g sugar
50g cracked black peppercorns
125ml dry white wine
handful shaved hickory wood chips (optional)

for the redcurrant sauce
zest of 2 oranges
60ml port
4 tablespoons redcurrant jelly
½ teaspoon cracked black peppercorns
60ml vegetable stock

Whisk together the egg yolks and the cider vinegar, then slowly add the walnut oil, whisking constantly. Season to taste with salt and pepper. Slice the apples and mix with the celery and walnuts in a bowl, then pour over the dressing and toss together. Set aside in the fridge.

Score the chicken skin with a few criss-cross lines, then stick the thyme stalks into the splits in the chicken skin. Lay the fillets out on a tray and sprinkle over the salt, sugar and cracked pepper. Pour the white wine over the top, cover then chill in the fridge for about 6 hours. Meanwhile place the wood chips in a jug with some warm water and allow them to soak up the water for about 6 hours.

Preheat the oven to 200°C (gas mark 6). Lay a wire rack inside a large roasting tin and scatter the wood chips into the tin under the rack (if using). Cover the tin with foil and place in the oven for about 20 minutes.

Remove the chicken from the fridge and run under cold water until all the salt, pepper and sugar is washed off. Take the roasting tin from the oven and remove the foil. Lay the chicken on the rack, re-cover with foil and place back in the oven for about 20 minutes or until the chicken is cooked through. Rest the chicken for a few minutes without removing the foil, then slice each breast into about 5 pieces.

Combine the orange zest, port and redcurrant jelly in a small saucepan. Add the black pepper and the vegetable stock, then bring to the boil. Cook for about 3 minutes, stirring constantly until the sauce is smooth. Serve the chicken pieces over a pile of the Waldorf salad with a little redcurrant sauce drizzled over.

Chilled chicken stuffed with fig and plum
on peach and cherry Sauvignon Blanc salad

OK, so it's a bit of a mouthful, but a good one at that! So often ignored as condiments and complements, fruits such as figs, plums and peaches have always been welcome on the national palate of Australia.

Serves 4	for the stuffed chicken	for the salad
	2 fresh figs	4 peaches
	250ml light rum	250g fresh cherries, stoned
	1 litre water	300ml Sauvignon Blanc white wine
	1 teaspoon black peppercorns	50g caster sugar
	100g caster sugar	1 cinnamon stick
	1 bay leaf	zest of ½ orange
	2 ripe dessert plums	zest of 1 lime
	4 skinless, boneless chicken breasts	
	salad cress to garnish	

Remove the hard portion from the base of the figs, then cut the figs into quarters. Put them in a bowl, pour over the rum and leave to soak for about 2 hours.

Strain the figs and set them aside, then pour the rum into a large saucepan with the water and add the peppercorns, sugar and bay leaf. Bring this mixture to the boil, then turn down the heat to just under simmering temperature, stirring until the sugar has dissolved. Cut the plums in half, remove the stones, then cut the halves again.

Cut a pocket into each chicken breast and stuff the plum and fig pieces into each pocket. Carefully place the stuffed chicken breasts in the rum poaching liquor and cook gently for about 20 minutes or until the chicken is cooked right through. Leave the chicken in the poaching liquid until cooled, then transfer to a dish, cover and chill completely in the fridge. Remove the chicken from the poaching liquor once cold.

Gently drop the peaches into a pan or heatproof bowl of boiling water and blanch for 20 seconds. Lift out using a draining spoon, then peel the peaches using a paring knife. Slice the fruit and discard the stones. In a large bowl, combine the peach slices with the cherries, cover and set aside.

Heat the wine with the sugar, cinnamon stick and orange zest in a saucepan over a medium heat for about 10 minutes, then remove from the heat and allow to cool. Add the lime zest, then pour the cooled, spiced wine over the peaches and cherries, stir and leave in the fridge for about 2 hours.

To serve, arrange a pile of the peaches and cherries on each plate, then slice the stuffed chicken breasts and arrange over the salads. Scatter with salad cress to garnish.

Cold chicken Maryland
with macadamia stuffing, tomato relish and marinated asparagus

Serves 4

for the tomato relish
250g ripe tomatoes, diced
75g brown onions, diced
1¼ teaspoons salt
60ml malt vinegar
75g sugar
¼ teaspoon curry powder
½ teaspoon mustard powder

for the marinated asparagus
32 asparagus spears, trimmed
60ml red wine vinegar
125ml olive oil
2 tablespoons capers
200g block good-quality
  Parmesan cheese
200g feta cheese

for the cold chicken Maryland
4 whole chicken legs, skin on
85g macadamia nuts
1 onion, finely diced
100g fresh breadcrumbs
2 tablespoons chopped fresh thyme
225g butter, melted
85g brown sugar
salt and pepper to season
lettuce leaves to serve

For the relish, combine the tomato and onion in a bowl, season with the salt and leave to stand overnight. The next day, drain off the juice and place the solids in a saucepan. Add the vinegar and cook for 30 minutes over a low heat. Add the sugar and spices, then cook for a further 30 minutes. Remove from the heat, cool then tip into a dish and chill in the fridge.

Gently lift the edges of the skin on the chicken to make a pouch for the stuffing. In a food processor, crush the macadamias into rough crumbs. Tip out into a bowl and add the onion, breadcrumbs and thyme. Add half the melted butter to the mixture, then season with salt and pepper. Blend together using your hands, adding more butter if needed to form a paste.

Preheat the oven to 180°C (gas mark 4). Place a ball of stuffing into each chicken 'pouch', pressing gently to force the stuffing under the skin. Baste the skin with the remaining melted butter and sprinkle with the brown sugar. Place the chicken in an ovenproof dish and bake for 25 minutes or until cooked through. Cool, then chill in the fridge for at least 3 hours.

For the asparagus, preheat the oven to 150°C (gas mark 2). Lay the spears in an ovenproof dish. Pour over the red wine vinegar and the olive oil and sprinkle the capers over the top. Cover, then bake for about 10 minutes, until just tender. Remove from the oven, cool, then chill in the fridge for about 1 hour, until cold.

Serve the chicken on a bed of lettuce, with a dipping bowl of tomato relish. Remove the asparagus from the marinade and drain, then serve as bundles on each plate. Scatter shavings of Parmesan and crumble the feta cheese over the top.

barbecue glory

Smoked salmon on shrimp, sweet chilli and spring onion blinis

Beer-battered flathead tails with preserved lemon & balsamic vinegar

Lemon and pepper tuna kebabs with crisp julienne salad

Australian steak sandwich with char-grilled potato chips

Warm Australasian beef salad

Steak stuffed with veal and garlic farce, served on penne with gremolata

Warm Cajun chicken with barbecued corn, celery and chickpea salad

Chicken stuffed with fresh sage, pesto and prosciutto

Marinated pork skewers on warm bok choy salad

Pork steak with homemade spicy plum sauce

Dukkah-crumbed buffalo escalopes with pepper sauce and Tabbouleh

Traditional Aussie beef burgers with the lot

Smoked salmon on shrimp, sweet chilli and spring onion blinis

I guess there had to be a shrimp on a barbeque hiding somewhere! The addition of shrimp to the blinis puts a subtle spin on an old favourite. Australian barbecues mainly include a flat plate for cooking on, but if you don't have one, the blinis can be cooked on a griddle or in a large, heavy-based frying pan.

Serves 4

400g smoked Atlantic salmon

for the blinis
125ml milk
¼ teaspoon easy-blend dried yeast
100g plain flour, sifted
2 eggs, separated
50ml double cream
100g small cooked shrimp, finely chopped
50ml Thai sweet chilli sauce
2 spring onions, finely chopped
2 tablespoons chopped fresh dill
100g unsalted butter for frying

for the mayonnaise
2 egg yolks
40ml cider vinegar
120ml vegetable oil
salt and pepper to taste

to serve
rocket leaves
capers
small sprigs of fresh dill

Warm 50ml of the milk to a tepid temperature in a jug or small bowl, stir in the yeast and 25g of the flour, then leave in a warm, draught-free place for about 15 minutes until doubled in volume.

Meanwhile, prepare the mayonnaise. Whisk the egg yolks and vinegar together in a bowl until light and fluffy, then slowly drizzle in the oil, whisking constantly until a mayonnaise has formed. Season to taste and set aside.

To complete the blinis, sift the remaining flour into a large bowl. Warm the remaining milk and add it to the flour with the frothy yeast liquid and the egg yolks, and stir until well combined. Whisk the egg whites until they form stiff peaks, then fold them into the yeast mixture with the cream, shrimp, sweet chilli sauce, spring onions and dill.

On a hot area of the flat plate, melt a little of the butter and place large spoonfuls of the mixture, leaving room for the blinis to spread. Fry for 2-3 minutes on each side until cooked through and golden. Cook all the mixture to make 8 blinis.

To serve, top half the blinis with a loosely folded strip of smoked salmon and some rocket leaves, then top each one with a second blini and more smoked salmon. Garnish with capers and little sprigs of fresh dill, grind over some pepper and drizzle the mayonnaise.

Beer-battered flathead tails
with preserved lemon & balsamic vinegar

Handled gently, this fish in beer batter cooks beautifully and has a light, delicate flavour that suits summer eating. In fact, you'll never want to eat deep-fried fish again. Large plaice fillets will make a perfectly good substitute for the flathead tails.

Serves 4

4 large flathead tails, filleted, cleaned and boned

for the beer batter
2 egg yolks
400ml draught beer
25ml vinegar
250g self-raising flour
100g flour for dusting

to serve
100ml balsamic vinegar
400g baby spinach leaves
60ml olive oil
50g preserved lemon, chopped
lemon wedges to garnish

Bring the balsamic vinegar to the boil in a small saucepan and boil until reduced by half. Set aside in a small jug until ready to serve.

Whisk the egg yolks together and add the beer and vinegar, then whisk in the flour to make a batter with a thick coating consistency. Roll the fish in the dusting flour, then dip in the batter and shake off the excess.

Heat the flat plate on the barbecue and grease well with vegetable oil, then cook the fish for about 2 minutes on each side, until the batter is crisp and golden brown on both sides.

To serve, pile the spinach leaves on serving plates and lay the battered fish alongside. Drizzle first with olive oil, then the reduced vinegar and then sprinkle with the chopped preserved lemon. Garnish with fresh lemon wedges.

Lemon and pepper tuna kebabs
with crisp julienne salad

Serves 4

for the kebabs
800g fresh tuna, cut into large cubes
2 tablespoons freshly cracked black peppercorns
grated zest and juice of 4 lemons
lime wedges to garnish

for the dressing
2 egg yolks
30ml lemon juice
100ml vegetable oil
salt and pepper to taste

for the salad
200g carrot, cut into julienne
200g mixed red and green pepper, cut into julienne
100g leek, cut into julienne
50g Spanish onion, cut into julienne

Thread the tuna cubes onto 8 skewers and lay in a shallow dish. If using wooden skewers, soak them first in water for 1 hour to prevent them from burning when put on the grill. Combine the pepper with the lemon juice and zest, pour over the tuna skewers and leave to marinate for about 30 minutes.

Meanwhile make the salad. Combine the egg yolks and lemon juice in a bowl and whisk well together. Slowly drizzle in the vegetable oil and whisk constantly until completely combined. Season to taste with salt and pepper. Combine the carrot, peppers, leek and onion and toss with the dressing.

Lightly oil the barbecue rack, then place the tuna skewers on the rack and grill for about 4 minutes, turning from time to time so they are cooked but still pink in the middle. Serve the kebabs with the salad and garnish with lime wedges.

Australian steak sandwich with char-grilled potatoes

The classic Aussie steak sandwich made on the barbecue packs a punch when it comes to taste and flavour. Sirloin or rib-eye steaks are often called 'Porterhouse' steaks in Australia, the mere mention of which gets any meat-lover's mouth watering!

Serves 4

50g butter
8 thick slices of crusty bread
4 x 200g sirloin or rib-eye steaks
4 potatoes, cut into 1cm thick slices and par-boiled
1-2 tablespoons vegetable oil
2 onions, finely sliced
4 rashers rindless bacon
8 quail's eggs
1 cos lettuce, finely sliced
2 tomatoes, sliced
4 slices Swiss emmenthal cheese
salt and pepper to taste

Butter the slices of bread and beat the steaks out to about 1cm thickness using a meat mallet.

Lightly toss the par-boiled potatoes with the oil, then slowly char-grill both the potatoes and onions on a griddle until the onions start to caramelise and the potatoes turn golden and crispy on the outside. Sprinkle with salt and pepper to taste. Wrap in foil or pop in the oven to keep warm.

Grill the bacon on the barbecue until it is crispy. Place to the side, then grill the steaks to medium-rare. Fry the eggs, sunny-side up on the flat plate or in a frying pan. Toast the buttered bread on both sides on the barbecue rack.

Layer the bread with lettuce, top with the bacon, steak and tomato then the onion and cheese. Finish each sandwich with two of the fried quail's eggs. Serve the potato chips onto plates alongside the grilled steak sandwiches.

Quail eggs can usually be purchased at country markets and make a fantastic
change to the standard chicken egg.

Warm Australasian beef salad

This to-die-for beef salad combines various Oriental ingredients, and has a relaxed, informal sense of occasion about it. The water chestnuts, baby corn and cashew nuts help give a lovely, crunchy texture to the salad.

Serves 4

for the marinade
2 fat fresh red chillies, deseeded and finely sliced
3 tablespoons chopped fresh coriander
3 garlic cloves, crushed
125ml ketchup manis (thick Indonesian soy sauce)
125ml oyster sauce

for the salad
750g rump or sirloin steak, cut into strips
2 red peppers, deseeded and finely sliced
1 onion, finely sliced
200g baby corn, cut into thirds
200g water chestnuts
200g bamboo shoots
300g baby spinach leaves
200g cashew nuts, toasted

Combine all the marinade ingredients in a large dish. Add the beef, peppers and onion, toss to coat thoroughly, then leave to marinate for at least 3 hours.

Cook the baby corn in a pan of boiling water for 3 minutes. Add the water chestnuts and the bamboo shoots to the cooking water to warm through.

Remove the beef, peppers and onions from the marinade. Place the beef, peppers and onions on the flat plate (griddle) and grill for 4 to 5 minutes until tender.

Put the spinach leaves in a large serving bowl, add the grilled beef, peppers and onions, the drained, warm vegetables and the cashews. Toss together and serve immediately.

Steak stuffed with veal and garlic farce
served on penne with gremolata

Serves 4

for the steak
250g veal, finely minced
2 tablespoons chopped fresh thyme
3 garlic cloves, crushed
4 x 200g sirloin or rib-eye steaks

for the pasta
300g dried penne (pasta quills)
125ml olive oil
2 tablespoons chopped fresh basil
salt and freshly cracked black pepper

for the gremalota
shredded zest of 1 large lemon
3 tablespoons chopped fresh parsley
3 tablespoons freshly grated Parmesan cheese

Combine the minced veal with the chopped thyme and crushed garlic. Cut a pocket in each of the steaks, then stuff each one with a quarter of the veal farce and secure with cocktail sticks or tooth picks.

Put a large saucepan of water on to boil. Meanwhile, combine the gremolata ingredients and set aside.

Place the steaks on the well-oiled barbecue rack, on a high setting over the coals, and gently grill them for 15 to 20 minutes, turning halfway through. Be sure to cook them to well done to ensure the stuffing is thoroughly cooked through.

When the steak is turned, after about 7 to 10 minutes, add the pasta to the boiling water and cook for 10 to 12 minutes until it is al dente. Drain and toss the pasta in the olive oil and basil, then season to taste.

Serve the pasta on plates, each topped with a steak. Sprinkle each steak with some of the gremolata.

Warm Cajun chicken
with barbecued corn, celery and chickpea salad

So often. cold salads can be repetitive in theme, however this a great example of combining popular flavours that make for a refreshing, tasty bite perfect for the summer months.

Serves 4

4 skinless, boneless chicken breasts

for the Cajun marinade
1 teaspoon chilli powder
1 teaspoon cayenne pepper
½ teaspoon dried thyme
½ teaspoon garlic powder
½ teaspoon onion powder
½ teaspoon salt
½ teaspoon cracked black pepper
4 tablespoons tomato purée
175ml vegetable oil
½ teaspoon Tabasco sauce

for the salad
2 corn cobs
25g butter, melted
2 celery sticks, chopped
2 Spanish onions, chopped
1 cucumber, deseeded and chopped
400g can chickpeas, drained and rinsed

for the mayonnaise
3 egg yolks
25ml cider vinegar
salt and pepper to taste
200ml vegetable oil

Cut the chicken into thick strips. Combine all the cajun marinade ingredients. Place the chicken in the marinade, turn to coat all over, then cover and leave for 1 hour in the fridge.

Brush the corn cobs with the melted butter, then wrap them in foil and place on the barbecue rack. Grill for about 15 minutes, turning regularly. Meanwhile combine the celery, onion, cucumber and chickpeas for the salad. Once the corn has finished cooking, remove the foil, peel off the outer leaves and gently slice down the side of the cobs with a sharp knife to remove the corn kernels. Mix these corn kernels into the salad.

Thread the chicken onto skewers, then grill slowly for 10 to 15 minutes until cooked through. While they are cooking, make the mayonnaise. Whisk the egg yolks, vinegar and salt and pepper until they are thick and creamy. Then, start to drizzle the oil into the mixture and whisk constantly until it is combined.

Stir the mayonnaise into the salad, then serve with the warm, grilled chicken skewers. If liked, serve with barbecued corn cobs.

Chicken stuffed with fresh sage, pesto and prosciutto

The pesto and prosciutto stuffing not only infuse their hallmark flavours into the chicken, but also help retain moisture throughout the meat.

Serves 4

4 slices prosciutto, thinly sliced
4 x 200g chicken breasts, butterflied

for the pesto
2 tablespoons chopped fresh sage
50g pine nuts, toasted
2 tablespoons chopped fresh basil
125ml olive oil
40g Parmesan cheese, grated
2 tablespoons crushed garlic

for the dressing
100ml olive oil
30ml balsamic vinegar
1 tablespoons wholegrain mustard
salt and freshly cracked black pepper

to serve
1 aubergine
1 courgette
3 tablespoons vegetable oil
salt and pepper to taste
400g baby spinach leaves

Combine all the pesto ingredients in a food processor and blend on pulse, leaving it quite chunky.

Lay the prosciutto slices out in the centre of the chicken breasts and fold if necessary so that none of it hangs out from the side of the breasts. Spoon the pesto evenly into the breasts, then fold the breasts over the filling.

Grill the chicken breasts on a well-oiled barbecue rack for about 8 minutes on each side or until the thickest part of the chicken is cooked through. Meanwhile, slice the aubergine and courgette into strips lengthways, dip in the vegetable oil and also grill on the barbecue rack or on a griddle. Season with salt and pepper.

Whisk together the olive oil, balsamic vinegar and mustard for the dressing and season with salt and pepper.

Serve the grilled vegetables and fresh baby spinach leaves with the grilled chicken and drizzle over the balsamic dressing.

Marinated pork skewers on warm bok choy salad

Bok Choy is loaded with vitamins, minerals and various antioxidants, and its subtle flavours perfectly underpin the marinated pork. Such Oriental vegetables are extremely popular in Australia these days and invariably add a fresh, tasty and nutritious element to so many dishes.

Serves 4

750g pork fillet (tenderloin),
   sliced into strips

for the marinade
125ml vegetable oil
125ml cider vinegar
125ml apple juice
½ teaspoon ground cloves
½ teaspoon ground cinnamon
½ teaspoon ground nutmeg

for the salad
100g butter
1 leek, roughly chopped
300g bok choy, separated into leaves
200g bean sprouts
60ml water
salt and pepper to taste

to garnish
½ leek, cut into julienne

Thread the sliced pork fillet onto 12 skewers and lay them in a dish. Combine all the marinade ingredients in a bowl and whisk together. Pour the marinade over the pork skewers, then cover and leave them in the fridge for 1 to 2 hours.

Once marinated, grill the kebabs on the barbecue for 10 to 15 minutes, turning them from time to time, until well cooked.

Meanwhile, get a wok very hot on the hob or char-grill, then add the butter and vegetables for the salad. Pour in the water, cover with a lid and steam for about 1 minute, then remove the lid and continue to cook for a couple of minutes until the vegetables are tender.

To serve, heap a pile of the warm bok choy salad onto each plate, then rest 3 skewers per serving on each salad. Garnish with a little leek, cut into julienne.

Pork steak with homemade spicy plum sauce

Serves 4

4 thick, boneless pork loin steaks

for the sauce
150g fresh plums, stoned and roughly chopped
40g brown sugar, or to taste
1 dessert apple, peeled, cored and roughly chopped
30ml brandy
50ml water

to serve
tossed leafy salad with roughly chopped tomatoes

Place all the sauce ingredients in a saucepan, stir well then cover and leave to cook on a gentle heat for 10 to 15 minutes or until the apple and plums are well-softened and able to be mashed. Remove the pan from the heat and using a potato masher, crush the fruit, leaving the sauce fairly chunky. Return to a very low heat and cover to keep warm.

Grill the pork steaks on the barbecue for 4 to 5 minutes on each side, until cooked through.

Serve the steaks with a generous helping of the fresh plum sauce and with the tossed green salad alongside.

Dukkah-crumbed buffalo escalopes
with pepper sauce and Tabbouleh

Of Middle-Eastern origins, Dukkah seasoning is a spicy, dry dip made with nuts. Traditionally served as a condiment with bread, Dukkah also makes a superb seasoning for various meats, including fish. Experiment with your favourite spices to add some personal flair.

Serves 4

800g buffalo fillet
  (or topside, thick flank or rump)
75g flour
4 egg yolks

for the Tabbouleh
200g bulghur wheat
500ml boiling water
2 large tomatoes
2 tablespoons chopped fresh mint
25g fresh parsley, chopped
2 spring onions, thinly sliced
85ml lemon juice
60ml olive oil
1 teaspoon salt
1 teaspoon pepper

for the pepper sauce
1 small onion, finely diced
½ tablespoon fresh red and pink peppercorns,
  crushed
½ tablespoon fresh green peppercorns,
  crushed
½ tablespoon mixed dried peppercorns,
  coarsely crushed
60ml brandy
250ml double cream

for the dukkah
½ teaspoon onion salt
½ teaspoon garlic salt
¼ teaspoon chilli powder
1 tablespoon dried mixed herbs
½ tablespoon sesame seeds
½ tablespoon poppy seeds
100g pine nuts
½ teaspoon mustard seeds, crushed
50g fine dried breadcrumbs
½ teaspoon coriander seeds, crushed

Place the bulghur wheat in a large heatproof bowl and pour on the boiling water. Cover and leave for about 20 minutes or until the water has been absorbed. Meanwhile, cut the tomatoes in half and remove the seeds, then cut the flesh into 1cm cubes. Mix the tomatoes, mint, parsley and spring onions together. In a separate bowl, combine the lemon juice, olive oil, salt and pepper. Drain the bulghur and squeeze out any excess water, then place back in the bowl and add the tomato and herb mixture. Pour over the lemon and oil dressing, then mix thoroughly.

Cut the meat into 100g slices, then beat each slice out gently with a meat mallet until it is fairly thin. Meanwhile, use a food processor to combine all the dukkah ingredients and blend until fine, or grind in a mortar and pestle and mix to an even consistency. Tip onto a large plate.

Dip the escalopes in the flour, then the egg yolk, then coat with the dukkah mix to completely cover. Set aside while preparing the pepper sauce.

In a small saucepan, cook the onion gently with the assorted peppercorns. Once the onion has softened, add the brandy (being careful of the flambé effect), then immediately add the cream and bring to the boil. Cook until the cream has reduced by half and the sauce is fairly thick. Season to taste with a little salt. Remove and set aside.

Lightly oil the barbecue rack, then grill the escalopes for 2 to 3 minutes on each side until they are golden brown. Serve the escalopes heaped together with the Tabbouleh and with the pepper sauce drizzled over.

Traditional Aussie beef burgers with the lot

The traditional Aussie beefburger is a nostalgic favourite across the country. They are a great idea for outdoor parties, where everyone can mix and match accompaniments as they please. The peanut butter is a must - you'll know why when you try it.

Serves 4

for the burgers
800g finely minced beef
75g peanut butter
75ml Worcestershire sauce
75ml tomato ketchup
salt and pepper to taste
3 eggs
50g fresh breadcrumbs

to serve
4 eggs
4 large round crusty rolls
1 lettuce, shredded
4 large slices of Swiss cheese
2 tomatoes, sliced
4 pineapple rings
8 large slices of beetroot

Place the mince in a large bowl. Add the peanut butter, Worcestershire sauce, tomato ketchup and salt and pepper. Mix roughly by hand until the ingredients are well combined. Add the 3 eggs and mix again, slowly adding the breadcrumbs until the mixture holds together. Divide the mixture into 4 and shape into 10cm flat patties.

Grill the burgers on a lightly oiled barbecue rack for about 8 minutes on each side until well-cooked all the way through. Meanwhile, fry the 4 eggs sunny-side up in a frying pan, until the whites are cooked and the yolks are just starting to set.

Split the rolls open and dress with your chosen accompaniments, then place the burgers and fried eggs in the rolls and serve at once.

afternoon tea & dessert favourites

Champagne mousse with strawberries

Strawberry and mango Pavlova with zabaglione

Mocha pannacotta with Irish cream liqueur

Chocolate almond pudding with chocolate cream sauce

Pecan dumplings with honey syrup

Baked chocolate ricotta cheesecake

Macadamia and golden syrup tartlets

Raspberry meringue pie

Ebony and ivory chocolate tart

Sweet potato, rum and pumpkin pie

Lamingtons

ANZAC biscuits

Champagne mousse with strawberries

Serves 4

for the macerated fruit
500g strawberries, hulled and quartered
300ml Champagne
125ml water
225g caster sugar

for the mousse
250ml double cream
5 eggs, separated
115g caster sugar
300ml Champagne
2 teaspoons powdered gelatine
2 tablespoons hot water

Put the prepared strawberries into a large heatproof bowl. Pour the Champagne and water into a large saucepan, bring to the boil, then boil rapidly until reduced by half. Reduce the heat, stir in the sugar and simmer gently, stirring until the sugar has dissolved and the mixture is turning into syrup. Don't overcook or brown the syrup. Pour the syrup over the strawberries, allow to cool, then chill in the fridge for at least 2 hours.

Lightly whip the double cream, then cover and put back in the fridge. Combine the egg yolks and sugar in a heatproof bowl and whisk thoroughly using an electric hand whisk until pale and creamy. Whisk the Champagne into the mixture. Place the bowl over a pan of simmering water (the base of the bowl should not touch the water) and cook gently, whisking constantly for about 10 minutes or until the mixture thickens to a nice mousse consistency. Remove from the heat and continue whisking for about 1 minute.

Stir the gelatine into the hot water in a small bowl, then heat gently in the microwave for a few seconds, without boiling, just until the gelatine has completely dissolved. Whisk the dissolved gelatine into the Champagne mixture, then allow the mixture to cool in the fridge for 15 minutes before continuing.

Meanwhile, whisk the egg whites in a clean grease-free bowl to form soft peaks. Fold the whipped cream, then the whisked egg whites into the chilled Champagne mixture, then pour the mousse into individual glasses. Chill in the fridge for about 6 hours until set. Serve the mousses with some of the macerated strawberries to decorate.

Strawberry and mango Pavlova with zabaglione

Of all the friendly rivalries that exist between Aussies and Kiwis, the question of "who invented Pavlova?" is an enduring one. Most Australians will tell you that 'Pav' was created in 1935 by chef Herbert Sachse, at the Hotel Esplanade in Perth, to celebrate a tour by the great Russian ballerina, Anna Pavlova. Suffice to say, this well-loved dish draws sighs of affection from both sides of the Tasman. The zabaglione makes a luscious counterpart to the marshmallow centre of the pavlova.

Serves 4

for the meringue
3 egg whites
175g caster sugar
¾ teaspoon white wine vinegar
pinch of salt
½ teaspoon cornflour

for the zabaglione
8 large egg yolks
115g caster sugar
125ml Marsala wine

for the fruit decoration
500g strawberries, hulled and quartered
3 mangoes, peeled, stoned and thinly sliced
300ml double cream, whipped

Preheat the oven to 140°C (gas mark 1). Cover a baking sheet with non-stick baking parchment. Whisk the egg whites in a clean, grease-free bowl until soft peaks form, then gradually whisk in the sugar, a couple of tablespoons at a time, with the vinegar, salt and cornflour, until smooth and glossy. Spoon the meringue into 6 even piles, roughly round and indented in the centre. Bake for 1 hour, then turn the oven off and leave the meringues in the oven for about another hour until completely cold.

To make the zabaglione, place the egg yolks in a heatproof bowl and whisk, using an electric hand-beater, until pale yellow. Whisk in the sugar, about ½ tablespoon at a time, whisking well after each addition. Whisk in the wine. Place the bowl over a pan of simmering water and whisk continuously over a low heat for about 10 minutes, until the mixture is thick and foamy. Ensure that the mixture does not boil at any point. Chill the zabaglione in the fridge for about 2 hours.

Mix together the quartered strawberries and slices of mango. To serve, divide the zabaglione among 4 bowls and float a meringue on the top of each. Spoon some of the whipped cream on top of each meringue, decorate with the fruit and serve at once.

Mocha pannacotta with Irish cream liqueur

This tastes just as good as it looks and sounds, and I don't know a soul who doesn't love Irish cream liqueur. This is a chocolate and coffee variation on the classic "cooked cream" recipe, and is extra appealing served with orange segments.

Makes 4

for the pannacotta
5 egg yolks
115g caster sugar
375ml double cream
60ml Irish cream liqueur
150g dark chocolate, broken into pieces
1 vanilla pod, split
1½ teaspoons powdered gelatine
30ml strong coffee (1 shot)

to decorate
orange segments
strips of orange zest cooked in sugar syrup

Combine the egg yolks, sugar, cream, liqueur and chocolate in a double boiler or a heatproof bowl over a pan of simmering water. Scrape the seeds from the vanilla pod into the mixture, then add the pod, too. Cook slowly, stirring the whole time, until the chocolate has melted and the mixture is starting to thicken as the egg yolks cook. Take off the heat and remove the vanilla pod.

Stir the gelatine into the hot coffee in a cup, then heat gently in the microwave for a few seconds, without boiling, just until the gelatine has completely dissolved. Stir the gelatine liquid into the chocolate cream mixture, then pour into four individual dariole (castle) moulds or ramekins.

Allow to cool, then place in the fridge and leave to set for at least 12 hours. To serve, run the tip of a knife around the edge of each pannacotta. Place an inverted serving plate over the top of each mould and turn them upside down, holding the two firmly together. Lift off the moulds. Serve chilled with orange segments and caramelised orange zest.

Chocolate almond pudding with chocolate cream sauce

The decoration here is called "Pashmak", which is similar to candy floss. Derived from sesame seeds, it has a sweet and slightly bitter flavour that adds a fresh dimension to the pudding.

Makes 4

for the pudding
450g blanched almonds
½ teaspoon cold water
30g caster sugar
½ tablespoon rosewater
150ml milk
2 eggs, separated
50g dark chocolate, grated

for the sauce
500ml double cream
280g dark chocolate, broken into pieces

to decorate
Pashmak (optional)

Preheat the oven to 180°C (gas mark 4). Grease four individual, dariole (castle) moulds or mini pudding basins. Crush the almonds in a food processor until they resemble a smooth paste, dripping the water over the almonds as you process them to prevent the oil from separating. Add the sugar and mix well, then add the rosewater, milk and egg yolks and mix again. Transfer to a large mixing bowl.

Whisk the egg whites in a clean, grease-free bowl until they form soft peaks, then using a large metal spoon, fold them through the almond mixture along with the grated chocolate. Divide the mixture evenly among the moulds or basins.

Place the moulds in a deep baking dish and pour boiling water around the edge to come halfway up the sides of the moulds/basins. Bake for 30 minutes or until the puddings are soft and springy to the touch.

Meanwhile, make the sauce. Heat the cream in a saucepan until it has almost reached boiling point. Remove the pan from the heat and add the chocolate, stirring constantly until the chocolate has melted.

Run a knife around the edge of the moulds to loosen the puddings, then turn them out into serving bowls. Serve covered with the warm, thick chocolate sauce and decorate with the Pashmak.

Pecan dumplings with honey syrup

Does this bring back fond memories of your mum's warm winter dessert of golden syrup dumplings? These are a little lighter, but still hit the spot with their nutty, sweet flavours.

Makes about 30

for the dumplings
75g chilled butter, diced
450g self-raising flour
150g pecans, finely chopped
3 eggs, lightly beaten
150ml milk, or as needed

for the syrup
1 litre water
450g granulated sugar
125g butter
4 tablespoons runny honey
4 teaspoons lemon juice

to decorate
finely chopped pecans

Rub the butter into the flour in a large mixing bowl using your fingertips. Stir in the pecans, then add the eggs and sufficient milk to mix into a soft dough. Roll the dough into about 30 even-sized, small balls and set aside.

Put all the syrup ingredients into a large saucepan and bring slowly to the boil, stirring until the sugar has dissolved. Reduce the heat to a gentle simmer, then carefully spoon the dumplings into the syrup. Cover the pan with a lid and simmer for 10 minutes.

Remove the lid and carefully turn the dumplings over. Replace the lid and simmer for a further 10 minutes until cooked through. Remove the dumplings using a draining spoon and serve in bowls with a little of the syrup poured over and decorated with a few more chopped pecans.

Baked chocolate ricotta cheesecake

The addition of chocolate into this old favourite will have everyone coming back for more. I prefer to use Dutch cocoa in this recipe for its strong, rich flavour.

Makes 4

100g sweet biscuits, crushed
450g ricotta cheese, strained
115g caster sugar
30g Dutch cocoa powder, sifted
2 tablespoons plain flour
2 teaspoons pure vanilla extract
3 egg whites
75g dark chocolate, roughly chopped

to decorate
whipped cream
dark chocolate shavings
a little cocoa powder, sifted

Preheat the oven to 160°C (gas mark 3). Sprinkle the biscuit crumbs over the base of four well-greased individual 10cm springform tins.

In a food processor, blend the strained ricotta cheese until it is smooth. Add the sugar, cocoa powder, flour and vanilla, then blend until just mixed. Transfer to a large mixing bowl. In a separate mixing bowl, whisk the egg whites to form soft peaks, then fold them with the chocolate pieces through the ricotta mixture using a large metal spoon.

Spoon the mixture into the individual tins, smooth the surface, then bake for about 30 minutes. The cheesecake is cooked when the edges are set. The centre may appear to be soft, but will set on standing. Turn off the oven and leave the door slightly ajar, then leave to rest in the oven for 1 hour, so as to cool slowly.

Put the cheesecakes in the fridge and leave for a further 1 hour or more until completely cold and set. Run a knife around the edge, then release the clip and remove from the tins. Slide a spatula or palette knife under the cakes and carefully remove the tin base.

To serve, top with whipped cream and chocolate shavings and dust with sifted cocoa powder.

Note: The cheesecakes can be made in one 22cm springform tin, although the cooking time needs to be doubled.

Macadamia and golden syrup tartlets

Makes 4

for the pastry
50g macadamia nuts, chopped
125g chilled butter, diced
1 egg
300g plain flour
50g icing sugar

for the filling
300g macadamia nuts, halved
2 eggs
115g caster sugar
85g light muscovado sugar
85g golden syrup
100g butter, melted
few drops of pure vanilla extract

to serve
a little icing sugar, sifted
vanilla ice cream

Preheat the oven to 160°C (gas mark 3). Process the macadamias for the pastry in a food processor until finely ground. Add the butter, egg, flour and icing sugar and pulse briefly to combine. Gently knead into a soft dough, then wrap in cling film and chill for 20 minutes before rolling out. Put the nuts for the filling on the baking sheet and roast in the oven for 10 minutes.

Roll out the pastry on a lightly floured work surface. Use to line four individual, loose-based 10cm tartlet tins. Line with greaseproof paper and weigh down with uncooked rice, then place on the baking sheet used for the nuts and bake 'blind' for 15 minutes. Remove the paper and rice, then set aside to cool while making the filling.

Beat the eggs in a mixing bowl, then add both the sugars, the golden syrup, butter and vanilla extract and beat well together. Add the roasted macadamia nuts and stir until combined.

Divide the filling mixture among the tartlet cases, then bake for 25 to 30 minutes or until golden. The pies will still be slightly wobbly in the middle when cooked, but the filling will firm up when the tartlets are cooled.

Remove the tartlets from the tins and serve either warm or cold, dusted with icing sugar and topped with vanilla ice cream.

Raspberry meringue pie

The tang of the raspberry filling strikes a heavenly match with the sweetness of the meringue, reminiscent of the old family favourite lemon meringue pie. The cream of tartar is an important element when preparing meringue as it helps stabilise the egg whites when whisking.

Serves 8

for the pastry
150g plain flour
50g icing sugar
75g chilled butter, diced
1 egg

for the meringue
4 egg whites
¾ teaspoon cream of tartar
115g caster sugar

for the filling
4 egg yolks
40g butter, softened
225g caster sugar
¼ teaspoon salt
5 tablespoons cornflour
5 tablespoons plain flour
1 teaspoon balsamic vinegar
250ml unsweetened raspberry purée
375ml water
175ml white wine

Sift the flour and icing sugar into a large mixing bowl. Add the butter, then rub the butter into the flour and sugar with your fingertips until well combined. Add the egg and gently knead together to form a smooth dough. Wrap tightly in cling film, then place in the fridge to chill for 20 minutes.

Preheat the oven to 200°C (gas mark 6). Roll out the pastry on a lightly floured surface and use to line a deep 25cm flan tin, with a removable base. Lay a sheet of baking paper over the pastry case, spread a cup of uncooked rice (or baking beans) over the surface so that it weighs the paper down and holds it in place. Bake for about 15 minutes or until the pastry is dry and very lightly browned. Remove from the oven, lift out the paper and rice, then leave to cool on a wire rack while preparing the filling. Reduce the oven temperature to 140°C (gas mark 1).

In a bowl, beat the egg yolks, butter, sugar and salt with the cornflour and plain flour. Add the vinegar and raspberry purée and mix well together. Combine the water and wine in a saucepan, then bring to the boil. Pour the hot liquid into the raspberry mixture, mixing well the whole time. Once all the ingredients are combined, pour back into the pan and cook very slowly for about 5 minutes over a low heat, stirring the whole time. Once the mixture has thickened and all the flour taste is cooked out, remove the pan from the heat. Allow the filling to cool for a few minutes, then pour it into the pastry case and spread evenly.

Whisk the egg whites with the cream of tartar until stiff, then gradually whisk in the sugar to make a thick glossy meringue. Spoon the meringue on top of the filling to cover evenly. Bake the tart for 20 to 30 minutes or until the meringue is golden. Allow to cool, then serve cut in slices. Serve with extra fresh raspberries, if liked.

Ebony and ivory chocolate tart

The layered white and dark chocolate in this tart will tempt any true chocoholic! This cake will make a rich and memorable finale to any meal, perfect with a strong black coffee or dessert wine.

Serves 12

for the chocolate pastry
150g plain flour, sifted
50g caster sugar
3 tablespoons Dutch cocoa powder
¼ teaspoon salt
85g chilled butter, diced
2 egg yolks
½ teaspoon pure vanilla extract

for the filling
500ml double cream
225g dark chocolate, broken into pieces
225g white chocolate, broken into pieces

to decorate
shavings of dark or milk chocolate

Preheat the oven to 180°C (gas mark 4) and put a baking sheet in the oven to heat. In a food processor, combine the flour, sugar, cocoa and salt and pulse briefly to blend. Add the butter and pulse again until fine crumbs form, then add the egg yolks and vanilla and pulse again briefly, just until the dough comes together.

Place the pastry dough into a lightly greased, deep 23cm loose-based flan tin and press evenly over the base and up the sides to the rim edge. Place the tin on the preheated baking sheet and bake for 18 to 20 minutes or until the pastry is cooked and looks slightly darker around the edges. Leave to cool for at least 1 hour.

Divide the cream evenly between two small saucepans. Gently heat both pans of cream until almost boiling, then remove from the heat and add the dark chocolate to one and the white chocolate to the other. Stir the mixtures until the chocolate has melted and the mixtures are smooth. Leave to cool for 5 minutes.

Carefully pour the white chocolate cream into the cooked pastry case. Then, carefully pour the dark chocolate cream on top of the white layer, being careful not to mix the two layers.

Allow the tart to set in the fridge for at least 12 hours (preferably 24 hours). Remove carefully from the tin, decorate with chocolate shavings and cut into about 12 even slices.

Sweet potato, rum and pumpkin pie

This is one of my favourite desserts to serve at parties. The sweet potato and pumpkin elements are a real eye-opener for many people – who said you can't have them in desserts? The cream, rum and spices lend a sophisticated delicacy to the pie.

Serves 8 to 10

for the pastry
175g flour
50g icing sugar
85g butter
1 large egg

to decorate
a little icing sugar, sifted

for the filling
225g sweet potato, steamed and mashed
225g pumpkin, steamed and mashed
115g light muscovado sugar
115g caster sugar
60ml white rum
¾ teaspoon salt
1½ teaspoons ground cinnamon
1½ teaspoons ground ginger
½ teaspoon ground cardamom
250ml double cream
2 large eggs

Sift the flour and icing sugar into a large mixing bowl. Add the butter, then rub it into the flour and sugar with your fingertips until well combined. Add the egg and gently knead together to form a smooth dough. Wrap tightly in cling film, then place in the fridge to chill for 20 minutes.

Preheat the oven to 200°C (gas mark 6). Roll out the pastry on a lightly floured surface and use to line a well-greased, deep 23cm loose-based flan tin. Reserve the pastry trimmings for a decoration. Lay a sheet of baking paper over the pastry case, spread a cup of uncooked rice (or baking beans) over the surface so that it weighs the paper down and holds it in place. Bake for about 15 minutes or until the pastry is dry and just very lightly browned. Remove from the oven, lift out the paper and rice, then leave to cool while preparing the filling. Reduce the oven temperature to 190°C (gas mark 5).

In a large bowl, mix together the sweet potato, pumpkin and muscovado sugar. Stir in the caster sugar and white rum, then add the salt, spices and cream and again, mix well. Add the eggs, one at a time, beating well after each addition. Pour the mixture into the pastry case, place the pie on a baking sheet, then bake for 1 hour. The filling is cooked when the pie has only a slight wobble in the centre when the pie is gently shaken.

While the pie is cooking, roll out the reserved pastry trimmings and cut out a decoration for the top of the pie. Lay on top of the pie, glazed with a little milk, for the final 15 to 20 minutes of the cooking time.

Allow the tart to rest for 15 minutes before cutting and serving warm, or allow to cool completely. Dust with sifted icing sugar and serve with whipped cream.

Lamingtons

These famous little treats are revered in Australia by young and old alike. You'd be hard pressed to beat a Lamington and a 'cuppa! Like many kids in Australia, I think the first thing I learned to bake was a Lamington for a "Lamington Drive" – for generations the fundraiser of choice for any self-respecting school or scout hall!

Makes 12

for the sponge cake
3 eggs
115g caster sugar
115g self-raising flour
40g cornflour
3 tablespoons hot water
15g butter
12 teaspoons strawberry jam

for the chocolate icing
500g icing sugar
40g Dutch cocoa powder
125ml milk
15g butter
250g desiccated coconut

to decorate
extra strawberry jam

Preheat the oven to 180°C (gas mark 4). Grease a 24 x 18cm cake tin and line the base with baking parchment. Beat the eggs and sugar in a large bowl, using an electric hand whisk, until the mixture is very thick and creamy. Sift together the self-raising flour and cornflour, then fold into the mixture using a large metal spoon. Stir the butter into the hot water until melted, then gently fold into the cake mixture.

Pour the mixture into the prepared cake tin and shake gently to spread evenly into the corners. Bake for 30 minutes or until golden brown and springy to the touch. Allow the cake to cool for about 5 minutes before turning out onto a wire rack to cool completely.

When cold, trim off any crusty outside edges, then cut the cake into 12 squares. Cut each square in half widthways, spread a teaspoon of the strawberry jam on each of the bottom layers, then place the top layers back on, to sandwich them together.

For the icing, start by sifting the icing sugar and cocoa into a heatproof bowl. Stir in the milk and butter, then place the bowl over a pan of simmering water and stir until the icing is smooth and glossy. Using a fork, dip each sponge square into the icing, then hold over the bowl to drain off any excess. Sprinkle well with the coconut then place on a baking tray to let the icing firm up before serving. Serve with a little strawberry jam spooned over the top of each Lamington, if liked.

Note: making the sponge cake the day before will make handling easier.

ANZAC biscuits

Like Lamingtons, the ever-popular ANZAC biscuit remains another old favourite for Australians. Originally baked for soldiers from the Australia and New Zealand Armed Corps, the recipe for ANZAC biscuits ensured the biscuit kept well during naval transport to the far-flung troops. Remember to bake them in volume - ANZAC biscuits have a habit of "disappearing" rather quickly!

Makes about 30
100g rolled oats
150g plain flour, sifted
225g caster sugar
65g desiccated coconut
125g butter
2 tablespoons golden syrup
½ teaspoon bicarbonate of soda
1 tablespoon boiling water

Preheat the oven to 150°C (gas mark 2). Line 2 baking sheets with baking parchment. Stir together the oats, flour, sugar and coconut in a large mixing bowl. Combine the butter and golden syrup in a small saucepan and stir over a gentle heat until the butter has melted. Mix together the bicarbonate of soda and boiling water and add to the melted butter mixture, then pour into the dry ingredients and mix everything well together.

Place about 30 teaspoonfuls of the mixture well apart on the baking sheets. Bake for 20 minutes or until the biscuits are golden brown. Leave to cool on the baking sheets for a few minutes, then transfer to a wire rack to cool completely.

Spiced butter, with date and walnut brunch loaf 35

Spinach:

    Potato, cottage cheese and spinach tart 80

    Kangaroo fillet served on beetroot pappardelle with smoked tomato
        and spinach 102–103

    Warm Australasian beef salad 139

Strawberries:

    Milk twists with brandied strawberry crush 36

    Champagne mousse with strawberries 156

    Strawberry and mango Pavlova with zabaglione 158

Sweet potato, rum and pumpkin pie 174

T

Tabbouleh, with Dukkah-crumbed buffalo escalopes with pepper sauce 150-151

Tarts:

    Sourcrust tarts with garlic shallots and balsamic mushrooms 45

    Potato, cottage cheese and spinach tart 80

    Macadamia and golden syrup tartlets 169

    Raspberry meringue pie 170

    Ebony and ivory chocolate tart 172

    Sweet potato, rum and pumpkin pie 174

Thyme:

    Mushroom, bacon and thyme omelette with peppery redcurrant sauce 18

Tomatoes:

    Tomato, olive and mushroom fry on outback flat damper 16

    Australian shearer's breakfast with Virgin Mary sauce 21

    Baked tomatoes stuffed with chicken and ham 23

    Flowerpot sun-dried tomato bread 76

    Braised steak on tomato and black-eyed bean salad 94

    Kangaroo fillet served on beetroot pappardelle with smoked tomato
        and spinach 102–103

    Crayfish salad with tomato, chervil and mange-tout 113

    Cold chicken Maryland with macadamia stuffing, tomato relish
        and marinated asparagus 126

Trout:

    Cured trout, pink peppercorn and brandy crêpe cake 64

Tuna:

    Thai tuna croquettes with coriander, chilli and lemongrass mayonnaise 57

    Roasted red pepper, aubergine and courgette with tuna and white bean salad 107

    Half-cured tuna on watercress salad with ginger and sesame dressing 116

    Lemon and pepper tuna kebabs with crisp julienne salad 134

V

Veal and garlic farce, with steak, served on penne with gremolata 141

W

Walnuts:

    Date and walnut brunch loaf with spiced butter 35

    Prune, apricot and walnut buns with ginger butter 38

    Smoked chicken on Waldorf salad with redcurrant sauce 123

Watercress:

    Half-cured tuna on watercress salad with ginger and sesame dressing 116

Y

Yoghurt:

    Warmed muesli with dried fruit and yoghurt 13

    Caramelised fruit salad with sweet mint yoghurt 14

    Lamb kefta with tzatziki and raisin couscous 75

Z

Zabaglione, with strawberry and mango Pavlova 158